THE
POETICAL WORKS
OF
JAMES MADISON BELL

AMS PRESS
NEW YORK

J. MADISON BELL

THE

POETICAL WORKS

OF

JAMES MADISON BELL

INCLUDING

" Creation Light "
The Dawn of Freedom
The Day and the War
The Triumph of Liberty
The Future of America

PRESS OF
WYNKOOP HALLENBECK CRAWFORD CO.
OF LANSING, MICHIGAN

Library of Congress Cataloging in Publication Data

Bell, James Madison, 1826-1902.
    The poetical works of James Madison Bell.

PS1085.B5 1973   811'.4   70-39423
ISBN 0-404-00005-3

811
B433 a

Reprinted from the edition of 1901, Lansing
First AMS edition published in 1973
Manufactured in the United States of America

AMS PRESS INC.
NEW YORK, N.Y. 10003

BISHOP B. W. ARNETT, D. D.

BIOGRAPHICAL SKETCH

OF

J. MADISON BELL

THE DISTINGUISHED ORIGINAL POET AND READER.

BY

BISHOP B. W. ARNETT, D. D.

———

The wealth of a nation does not consist alone in its bonds, gold, silver or lands, but the true wealth consists in the intelligence, courage, industry and frugality of the men, the intelligence, culture and virtue of its womanhood. Each generation produces its men and women for the times in which they live.

If it is war, warriors are produced. In case of law, judges and others are produced, so that the times, whether of an individual, family or race, very seldom calls for a man, that he is not to be found to lead on the armies, to teach its children, to encourage its people to renewed energy and effort. Our race is no exception to the general rule of history. During all of our sorrowful and sad history, we have had men and women when needed.

In contrasting the present time with the past there is great reason for encouragement, for at the close of the last century there was only one to sing our songs and weave the garland of poetry on the brow of the suffering race, or to offer laurels to the race who had won victories for the cause of human liberty and justice.

Phillis Wheatley was the morning star of the rising womanhood of the race, our first poet, and since that time we have had many who have enlivened our march by their music and encouraged our hearts by their words of inspiration and hope.

During the darkest hours of our bondage, during the time of the enforcement of the fugitive slave law, when the heavens were dark and clouds covered the sky, and there appeared to be no hope for the freemen of the North, or for the slaves of the South, all appeared to be lost, all avenues to opportunities were closed, in that sad hour Frances Ellen Watkins, the poetess of hope, like Miriam of old on the borders of the Red Sea, struck up the songs and notes, and sang,—

"Yes, Ethiopia yet shall stretch her bleeding
    hands abroad,
  Her cry of agony shall reach the burning throne
    of God."

Thus this song was sung in the home, in the school and in the church, and hope appeared to rise in the pathway of the coming generation and lightened the path of the children of despair.

When the heavens were threatening and many were faint of heart, then the bow of promise

spanned the western sky, it was during the dark
hours of our nation's history, it was then a new
star appeared above the horizon and a new
trumpet sounded, new notes were heard and the
vibrations of the sound reached from ocean to
ocean, it was then that the subject of our sketch
came upon the stage and became a lamp to our
feet and a light to our pathway.

James Madison Bell was born April 3, 1826,
at Gallipolis, Ohio. He lived there until he was
17 years of age. In 1842 he removed to Cincin-
nati, Ohio, and lived with his brother-in-law,
George Knight, and learned the plasterer's trade.
Mr. Knight was one of the best mechanics in the
city.

At the time of the arrival of Mr. Bell in Cin-
cinnati, the subject of education was agitated
among the colored and white people. The school
question was one of the living and burning ques-
tions, and had been since 1835. Previous to that
time the schools were private, taught by white
men for white children, but Mr. Wing and a
number of others allowed the colored youth to
attend the night schools. Peter H. Clark, in
speaking of the time that Mr. Bell came to Cin-
cinnati, uses the following language:

"A number of young men and women, filled
with the spirit of hatred to slavery, and a desire
to labor for a down-trodden race, came into the
city and established schools at various points,
one in the colored Baptist church on Western
Row, and was taught at various times by Messrs.
Barber, E. Fairchilds, W. Robinson and Angus
Wattles. Among the ladies there were the Misses
Bishop, Lowe, Mathews, and Mrs. Merrill. They
were all excellent teachers, deeply imbued with

a desire to do good, and are remembered with
gratitude by those who received instruction at
their hands. They were subject to much con-
tumely and abuse. Boarding-house keepers re-
fused to entertain them, placing their trunks upon
the sidewalk, and telling them that they had no
accommodation for 'teachers of niggers.' They
were obliged to club together and rent a house
and board themselves. Frequently the scholars
would be unable to meet regularly because of
mob violence. A part of the salaries of these
teachers was paid by an educational society, com-
posed of benevolent whites, many of whom sur-
vived to witness the triumph of principles which
they espoused amid such obliquy.

"A number of colored men co-operated heartily
in this work, among whom may be named Baker
Jones, Joseph Fowler, John Woodson, Dennis
Hills, John Liverpool, Wm. O'Hara and others.
These schools continued, with varying fortunes,
until 1844, when Rev. Hiram S. Gilmore, a
young man of good fortune, fine talents and rare
benevolence, established the Cincinnati high
school, which was, in some respects, the best
school ever established in the city for colored
people. Its proprietor, or rather patron, spared
no expense to make it a good success. Ground
was purchased at the east end of Harrison street,
and a commodious building of five large rooms
and a chapel was fitted up. Good teachers were
employed to instruct in the common branches of
an English course, besides which Latin, Greek,
music and drawing were taught."

The subject of our sketch was a busy man; he
worked by day and studied by night. He worked
at his trade in the summer and fall and studied

in the winter, each spring coming out renewed in strength and increased in knowledge. It was in these times that Mr. Bell entered school, and at the same time was indoctrinated into the principles of radical anti-slaveryism. It was in this school, in connection with Oberlin College, that the sentiment of Uncle Tom's Cabin was born in Walnut Hills, Cincinnati, giving an impetus to the cause of human freedom. Thus imbued and thus indoctrinated, he desired a wider field to breathe a freer atmosphere where his sphere of usefulness could be enlarged, which could only be enjoyed under the British flag.

In August, 1854, he moved with his family to Chatham, Canada, where he lived until 1860.

Mr. Bell was a personal friend of John Brown, of Harper's Ferry. He was a member of his counsel in Canada and assisted in enlisting men to go upon their raid. He was his guest while the recruiting was going on in Canada and was one of the last men to see John Brown when he left Canada for the United States. He only escaped the fate of many of John Brown's men by the providence of God.

He assisted in raising money to carry on the work, and is one of the last men now living who was personally connected with the Harper's Ferry raid. All honor to the men who gave aid, counsel and support to the hero of Harper's Ferry.

It was while in his twenty-second year that he courted and married Miss Louisana Sanderline, and to this marriage a number of children were born, who became useful men and women. In Canada he pursued his trade and was very successful and accumulated some money, but having a desire for a broader field, on the second day of

February, 1860, he started for California and
landed at San Francisco on the 29th of the same
month.

On arriving on the Pacific coast he found the
leaders of his race in an active campaign against
the disabilities of the children and the race in
that new country. He immediately became one
of them, and joined hands, heart and brain to
assist in breaking the fetters from the limbs of
his race in California and giving an equal oppor-
tunity for the people to acquire an education.

He was united on the coast with a noble band
of leaders; among them were Rev. T. M. D.
Ward, Darius Stokes, John J. Moore, Barnet
Fletcher, J. B. Sanderson, Rev. John T. Jennifer,
Richard Hall, F. G. Barbadoes, and Philip A.
Bell, editor of the Pacific Appeal.

Rev. James H. Hubbard, in speaking of the
pioneers of the gold coast, says they endured
many privations, chief among which were the
"lack of home comforts and influences." It had
been enacted in the laws of the golden state that
negroes were not permitted to testify in cases
where white men were the principals; the children
were denied admission to the common schools.
The people became aroused and held several
state conventions. At these conventions the lead-
ers of the race took an active part, and no one did
more than J. Madison Bell.

At the convention held by the ministers of the
African Methodist Episcopal church he took a
prominent part in the convention, united his in-
telligence and moral forces with the people. A
convention of ministers and laymen met Tuesday,
September 3, 1863, in San Francisco. Brother
Barney Fletcher called the meeting to order and

Elder T. M. D. Ward was appointed chairmen. In this convention they discussed the subjects of the church and state. We find Mr. Bell participating in the convention and is recorded as being a steward of the church at San Francisco. He was a member of the committees on finance and ministry, and their reports gave the proper keynote for ministerial education. He was on the committee on Sabbath schools and delivered several addresses before the people.

While in California, some of his most stirring poems were written. The poems on "Emancipation," "Lincoln," "The Dawn of Freedom," and the "War Poems" were all written while living at the Golden Gate. One of his finest poems is his "Valedictory on Leaving San Francisco." He left California and came back to the Atlantic states in 1865, just in time to fulfill his mission to the race by encouraging the new-born freedmen in their new duties and responsibilities.

He returned to Canada to visit his family, and after remaining for a short time he removed to Toledo, Ohio, and brought his family with him. For two years he traveled from city to city and proclaimed the truth and doctrines of human liberty, instructed and encouraged his race to noble deeds and to great activity in building up their newly-made homes.

It was during this period that I met him—and to meet him is to love him—and we became warm and true friends. From that day until now I have been one of his most ardent admirers, by reason of the congeniality of the man, of his intrinsic worth and his ability as a native poet.

His poetry is like the flowing of the mountain spring, the secret of its source is unknown. It

was not a well dug or bored, but a natural out-
flowing of the crystalline stream, which came
bubbling, sparkling, leaping, rolling, tumbling
and jumping down the mountain side, flowing
out over the plain like a silver brook on its jour-
ney towards the sea, furnishing water for thirsty
beast and man, power for mills and factories,
and life for the vegetable world. So it is with
the poems of Mr. Bell. They will be read by
the inhabitants of the mansion and hut, studied in
the school house, college and university, recited
in the parlor, lyceum, on the platform, and quoted
by pulpit and press.

During the years 1867 and 1868 in Cincinnati,
Ohio, night after night I accompanied him in his
readings; thence to Lockland, Glendale, Ham-
ilton and other places, where I had the pleasure
and satisfaction of witnessing some of the effects
of his poems. He read "Modern Moses" or
"Andrew Johnson Swinging Around the Circle"
with telling effect.

During these years of instruction, for he was
instructing the people of their political and civic
duties, they needed a teacher and leader, and no
one could have done it better than the manner
in which he presented it. It was like the music
that comes from the heavenly source. His poems
were read in all of the large cities of the North
and South, and many a young man who was not
an honor to his race and a blessing to his people
received the first spark of inspiration for true
greatness from hearing the poems of our sub-
ject.   In Washington, St. Louis, Baltimore,
Louisville, Atlanta and Charleston, the people
opened their arms and received the words after

beholding the star of hope as held out by the readings of our subject.

After traveling for several years he returned to Toledo, Ohio, where his family resided. His star rested over the city on the Maumee, and from that time until now he has been known as the "Bard of the Maumee."

He would follow his trade in the summer and fall, travel and read his poems during the winter—holding the trowel in one hand and his pen in the other. He was one of the best artists in his city and neighboring towns, always busy, calls more than he could fill for artistic work, though he labored hard, yet on going home in the evenings the muse would call him and a poem was born. Many of his brightest gems of thought were born on the scaffold and cradled in his wagon.

I have known him to sit down, and in a conversation some of the most beautiful expressions would come from his lips, thoughts that were crystallized, clothed in silken language, and were marshaled like an army on the battle field. His logic was irresistible, like a legion of cavalry led by Sheridan; troop after troop he would hurl against the logical battery of his opponent, whether in debate or speech, and the conclusion was shouts of victory heard above the music of the heart and the songs of the soul,

I was in the city of Toledo from 1870 to 1873. For three years I was his pastor. During my stay in the city he was the superintendent of the Sunday school. He never failed to do his duty, and he was present every Sunday. Frederick Douglas was a man like him. I remember while

in Chicago he said: "I make it a rule to go to
church and Sunday school once a day, that the
rising generation may know that Fred Douglas
is on the side of the church and Sunday school."

While living in Toledo, J. Madison Bell was
elected a delegate from Lucas county to the state
convention, and there he was elected as a delegate
at large from the state of Ohio to the national
convention, which met in Philadelphia, May,
1872. At this convention General Grant was re-
nominated for the presidency of the United
States. During the campaign his voice was heard
in many portions of the state, pleading for the re-
election of the hero of Appomattox.

His life has been one of great activity; his
services rendered to his race cannot be measured
by any standard that we have at our command.
His influences have been one of those subtile
influences. Like the atmosphere, it has gone
many places, and the people have felt and acted
upon it; they have become better and wiser by
reason of reading and hearing his speeches.

The honor of presenting an individual to a
select company, or to a distinguished audience, is
one privilege a man, perhaps, enjoys once in a life
time, but the privilege that is now afforded me
is of a very high order—the privilege of intro-
ducing an author and his book, not to a select
company of friends or to a high dignitary, but
to the commonwealth of letters, to the reading
and thinking men, women and children of the
present and future generations. The honor
carries with it a responsibility for the character of
the individual and the character of the book,
therefore I do not fear the consequence of the in-

troduction of so distinguished an individual or so useful a book.

I can endorse both, and feel it an honor to have the privilege of so doing, for if the book is to find its place in the reading circle of the world it will stand on its own merits; it will stand the examination of the most critical, whether friend or foe.

The book is a collection of the man—a busy man, a God-fearing man, a race-loving man, one who has spent the better part of his life in work and in study. The poems are the fruitage of his spare moments. I have long and persistently entreated my dear friend to have his poems collected and published. He has at last consented, and the work of compiling has been one of love and pleasure.

I therefore take great pleasure in introducing to the members of the commonwealth of letters, J. Madison Bell, "The Bard of the Maumee."

It was my pleasure and privilege to give a helping hand to Whitman's "Not a Man and Yet a Man," but in this introduction it gives me greater pleasure than I possess language to express.

In 1884 the general conference of the A. M. E church adjourned its session in Baltimore and was received at the white house by the President of the United States, Chester A. Arthur. It was my pleasure to present the bishops, general officers and members to his excellency, the President of the United States, an honor enjoyed by few. *This privilege of introducing one of my own race, of my own church and political faith, a man whose poems will stand as his monument*

*from generation to generation, and will give light
and joy to the laboring and struggling people for
many centuries.*

He will lighten their burden and illumine their
pathway, whether in religion or politics; he will
stand and present the "Banishment of Man from
the Garden of the Lord," and from all of its
effects he will hang the star of hope over the
gateway of Eden. To the many under op-
pression, he will stand to them the day of "Dawn
of Liberty," and to those who are fighting the
battles of the moral, religious and educational
interests, he will present them with the "Triumph
of Liberty" or "Creation Light."

Apostrophe of Time.

O fleeting Time! whence art thou come?
  And whither do thy footsteps tend?
Deep in the past where was thy home,
  And where thy future journey's end?

Thou art from vast eternity,
  And unto boundless regions found;
But what and where's infinity?
  And what know we of space unbound?

The furrowed brow betokens age;
  But who thy centuries can tell?
Was ancient seer or learned sage
  In wisdom's lore e'er versed so well?

Hast thou from childhood wandered thus,
  Companionless and lone, through space,
With mystery o'er thy exodus,
  And darkness 'round thy resting place.

What lengthened years have come and gone,
  Since thou thy tireless march began,
Since Luna's children sang at dawn,
  The wonders of creation's plan?

How many years of gloom and night
  Had passed, long ere yon king of day
Had reigned his fiery steeds of light,
  And sped them on their shining way?

Thou knowest—Thou alone, O thou!
   Omniscient and eternal Three!
To whose broad eye all time is now—
   The past, with all eternity;

In whose dread presence I shall stand,
   When time shall sink to rise no more,
In that broad sea of thy command,
   Whose waves roll on, without a shore.

(January 3, 1863.)

Creation Light.

Deep in the unrecorded past,
   There was an age of darkness vast,
   And boundless as the realms of space.
   An age that held, in its embrace
   And in an embryotic state,
All worlds and systems, small and great.

An inorganic age, a night
   In which no star or ray of light,
In all the myriad ages gone,
   Had rose or smiled that night upon.
A dismal, shoreless waste and void,
   Where nature, crude and unemployed,

A shapeless, heterogeneous mass
   Had lain for ages, that surpass
The numerate skill of all the line
   Of men or angels to define.

But when in spirit the mighty God
  Moved o'er the dark, abysmal flood,
And raised his omnific voice of might,
  And said to the deep, "Let there be light!"

Lo! a bright orb of deathless flame
  From out the womb of darkness came,
And ere the silence was restored,
  In radiant beams of light were poured
Upon a drear and cheerless waste,
  Where gloom and chaos had long embraced.

"Let there be light!" and God's first born,
  Clothed in the princely garb of morn,
Assumed his long pre-ordered place,
  And dropped the mantling from his face.

Grim darkness saw, and filled with dread,
  Her ebon pinions widely spread,
And flew, with terror-stricken fright
  Before the piercing beams of light.

"Let there be light!" and high in heaven,
  Sun, moon and stars, and planets seven,
Stood in their lots, moved in their spheres,
  And time began his march of years.

As nature lay immured in gloom,
  And rayless as the lifeless tomb,
Until the orient dawn of light
  Dispelled the darkness of the night.

E'en so, in ignorance groped mankind,
  Till reason's torch illumed the mind.
They saw the burning sun at noon,
  At night the ever-changing moon.

And saw the myriad stars, that blaze
    And fill, with their resplendent rays,
The deep nocturnal vaults on high,
    But never thought or questioned why.

Thought makes the man: 'tis thought that soars;
    Reason, the realms of thought explores.
Oh, reason! wondrous attribute,
    Thou land-mark drawn 'twixt man and brute,

Thou art creation's highest test,
    Her universal alchymist;
For by thy torch mankind may trace
    Nature e'en to her secret place,

And there, with meek, becoming pride,
    May cast the mystic veil aside;
May check the lightning in its speed,
    Make it subservient to his need;

Measure the sun as with a chain,
    Prognosticate the snow, the rain;
Distance the earth from pole to pole,
    And mark the seasons as they roll.

Oh, thou! eternal source of light,
    Ineffable and infinite,
Whom angels praise and saints adore,
    Whose glory is and was before.

Before the morning stars in songs sublime,
    Chanted the wondrous birth of time,
Whose glory is, was and shall be,
    When time has filled his destiny.

And when the orbit lamps above,
  Those burning children of thy love,
Shall fade from out the vaulted sky,
  And sun and moon and systems die;

Creation sink in rayless gloom,
  And night and chaos their reign resume,
Still wilt Thou all changeless be,
  God, Jehovah, Deity.

Admonition.*

Where e'er the fetter has been broken,
    Where e'er the bondsman has been
        freed,
    Where e'er a sentence has been spoken
    In behalf of human need—

Whether on towering, snow-capped mountain,
  Or in the soft and flowery vale,
Whether beside the gurgling fountain,
  Or 'long the streamlet's watery trail—

Whether amid the leafy wildness
  Of Bashan's sturdy oaks and pines,
Or 'midst the sheen and plastic mildness
  Where art presides and genius shines.

----

*This poem was delivered by the author at the Freed-
man's and Union Commission picnic, Park hotel
grounds, Alamed, Tuesday, May 15, 1866.

In grand effect they still are living,
    Unblurred by age or flight of time;
And unto earth are ever giving
    Lessons, wondrous and sublime.

Like trees of fadeless beauty growing,
    In all their grand omnific pride,
Whose fruits of life and joy bestowing,
    Have blest the land and blest the tide.

Those noble acts, through all the ages
    Have lived, all worthy to commend,
And the true historian's pages,
    With such, shall glow 'till time shall end.

For there's a link that binds together
    All the peoples of this our earth,
A band which nothing can dissever,
    The germ of man's primeval birth;

A deathless kinship—a relation,
    A brotherhood that knows no bounds,
Pervading earth in every station
    Where e'er the human form is found.

And there, without regard to nation,
    Without respect to birth or hue,
Man stands sublime in his creation,
    Begirt with freedom as his due.

The ox and yoke have some relation,
    As do the horse and curbing rein.
But, in the day of man's formation,
    He was not fashioned for the chain.

And nowhere, save through base perversion
  Of the grand "wherefore" he was made,
Has dark presumption's foul coercion
  E'er dared his freedom to invade.

That freedom which to him was given
  Ere Eden's first-born rose had died,
Or sin the human heart had riven,
  Or man his Maker had defied.

Given, and with it came dominion
  O'er all the fish that throng the sea,
O'er all the birds of downy pinion,
  O'er all the prowling beasts of prey;

And o'er the cattle wildly roving,
  And over every creeping thing;
And o'er the earth with God's approving
  Smile, man was crowned Creation's king.

And yet, in all this vast arrangement,
  In all the amplitude of plan,
No grant is found for the estrangement
  Whereby man lords it over man.

"I am the Lord!" said the Eternal.
  "Worship thou no God but me!
Nor in thy memory hold supernal
  Aught of all thy destiny."

And wheresoever an invasion
  'Gainst this injunction has been planned,
Heaven has made it the occasion
  For rendering bare his chastening hand.

And oh! how dire the retributions
   Which have followed evermore,
Intestine wars and revolutions
   Have drenched the earth with human gore.

Egypt and Greece and Rome and Carthage,
   This heaven injunction set at naught,
And where are they? The merest vestige
   Remains of all they proudly wrought.

Their rock-bound cities, whose proud basis
   Seemed all impervious to decay,
Time's mighty besum, that erases
   The pride of man, has swept away.

Nor has our birth-land been excepted,
   Her hundred fields all bathed in blood,
Bear the impress of truth rejected,
   And scourgings of an angry God.

The scourgings of a God whose justice
   And fearful judgments move apace,
And faithful ever in their office
   To vindicate an injured race.

Yes we have sinned and God has scourged us,
   And from his chastenings we are sore,
Oh! may the deep affliction urge us
   To live in peace and sin no more.

Beware! if God has built this nation,
   All its constituents are good
And needful to its preservation,
   Whether they be stone or wood.

We may not comprehend the structure
In full minutia and design,
Nor trace its varied architecture
In arris, groove and curve and line.

Be faithful and the great Grand Master
Will on his trestle-board make plain
All that's obtuse, but no whit faster
Than 'twere needful to explain.

But, we'll not pain the ear by telling
Of all the wrongs they have endured,
Of all the brutal, fiend-impelling
Outrage, to which they've been inured.

No, these shall form their own dark story,
The which, like spectres from the dust,
Shall haunt this nation, bruised and gory,
Till all her laws are pure and just.

Till there shall be no class restriction,
Her statutes free from every flaw,
Her native sons without distinction,
Stand equals all—before the law.

That those, from whom the chains are falling,
May be inspired with a zeal
Commensurate with the lofty calling,
Which every patriot heart should feel.

The chain, thank God! the chain is broken,
Its severed links may do us harm;
But the Grand Fiat has been spoken,
And free forever is the arm.

Though free from chains, yet there are thousands
  Poor, homeless, clotheless and unfed,
And these, in praying us to aid them,
  They plead the merits of their dead.

They plead their feeless toil and labor,
  Conducive to this nation's worth,
Whereby she stands today a neighbor,
  Courted by all the realms of earth.

And they plead the noble daring
  Of their two hundred thousand brave
Warriors, who with manly bearing
  Went forth, a struggling land to save.

And hence, their deathless claim upon us,
  Claims such as we can ne'er forego;
Ay, claims that truth doth urge upon us,
  The just assuagement of their woe.

Though poor they be, and very many,
  Their care and keeping's in our hands,
The rich man's pound, the poor man's penny,
  If not withheld when need demands.

But freely tendered and with kindness,
  To these, the long and sore oppressed,
Know that our land with heaven's benignness,
  In rich abundance shall be blest.

Though poor they be, yet their condition
  And of its wherefore, know we all,
We know the base of their petition,
  The truth and justness of their call.

Therefore, in view of all the sorrows;
   In view of all the grief and pain;
In view of all the nameless horrors,
   Foul emanations of the chain.

O let us toil with might unceasing,
   Until the land, which gave us birth,
Whose glorious sunlight is increasing,
   Becomes the flower of all the earth.

Until beneath her spreading pinions,
   And outstretched folds of liberty,
Men of all nations and dominions
   Shall dwell in peace and unity.

To this great end, then, let us labor,
   Knowing the fruits of our employ,
Shall raise up many a prostrate neighbor,
   And fill their grateful hearts with joy.

And then the "Union Aid Commission,"
   Whose worthy object is to bless
And change the hapless, sad condition
   Of all the sons of wretchedness,

Shall in its mission work a marvel,
   In seeking out the passing poor,
Of roofless cabin, hut and hovel,
   And blessings leave at every door.

O wondrous mission, high and holy!
   Never is labor so sublime
As when it seeks to lift the lowly,
   Without regard to class or clime,

And thus forgeteth self for others,
  And labors for a common good,
Regarding all mankind as brothers,
  And earth as one great neighborhood.

God bless that mission! may it prosper
  And spread its wings o'er land and seas,
Till like the gentle dews of vesper,
  Its joys are felt in every breeze.

———

The Black Man's Wrongs.

reathe softly on my harp, O Muse!
  In gentle strains now clothe its songs,
Thy all inspiring force infuse,
  While singing of the black man's
    wrongs.

Wrongs that defy the painter's skill,
  Nor can the tongue e'er tell them o'er,
They seem at first a tiny rill,
  And then a sea without a shore.

But here the feelings of the soul
  Defy the language of the tongue.
Therefore if we in part unroll
  The black man's wrongs, our task is done.

First view him in the Torrid Zone,
  Sporting amid luxurious groves
Where nature delveth all alone,
  And man in search of pleasure roves.

While there, his every meal was spread
  By genial nature's bounteous hand,
Where he from childhood's morn had fed,
  With all her gifts at his command.

At noon, beneath the spreading palm,
  Or prostrate in some shady bower,
His soul inhaled the fragrant balm,
  By zephyrs brought from fruit and flower.

No raging sea of sorrow there
  Had e'er their muddy billow swept
Over his soul's instilling fear,
  Nor had the man of pleasure wept.

But alas! this home was entered,
  Entered by Christians wise and bold;
Christians, whose great heart was centered
  On their nation's god of gold.

By Christians he was borne away,
  In fetters o'er the trackless main,
To where the gospel's blaze of day
  Looks smilingly on blood and pain.

Then begins a tale of weeping,
  A tale of rapine and of woe,
Only known to him that's keeping
  The record of man's acts below.

For since he crossed the rolling flood,
    And landed on Virginia's shore,
His path presents a scene of blood
    Unknown to history's page of yore.

His dearest friends are crushed and torn
    Asunder, ne'er to meet again.
Fettered and branded, gagged and borne
    Where moral death and darkness reign.

Their wailing cries afflict the ear,
    Their groans and sighs so pain the heart,
Till often the unconscious tear
    For these poor hapless, sad ones start.

'Tis not in mortal man to paint
    The damning scenes transacted there,
At thought of which the heart grows faint
    And clouds the brow with dark despair.

Were all the gags, bolts, bars and locks,
    The thumbscrews, handcuffs and the chain,
The branding-iron and the stocks,
    That have increased the Afric's pain,

Piled up by skillful smith or mason
    With care in one great concave heap,
Those gory gyves would form a basin
    Unnumbered fathoms wide and deep.

Could all their blood and tears alone
    Flow in this basin, deep and wide,
The proudest ship, the world hath known,
    Could on that basin's bosom ride.

And then, could all their groans and sighs,
    Their anguished wailings of despair,
But freight that ship, just where she lies,
    'Twould sink that mammoth vessel there.

Their blood and tears are treasured up
    Where all their sighs and groans are stored,
And will, from retribution's cup,
    Upon this guilty land be poured.

America, where is thy blush?
    Or, is thy very heart of stone?
Will not thy millions cease to crush
    The sable outraged few that groan?

Shall they, because their skins are dark,
    Forever wear the galling chain?
Has hope for them no cheering spark
    That wrong will one day cease to reign?

Thou great Goliath, stay thy frown!
    Boast not thyself in thy great strength,
The brooklet's stone may bring thee down!
    Thy sword may clip thy head at length!

Gone forth, long since, is the decree
    That binds my shattered hopes in one,
Though I shall sleep, yet time will be,
    What God has spoken, He will have done.

"Judgment is mine! I will repay!"
    Thus saith the builder of the sky,
Although his judgments still delay,
    With every sun they're drawing nigh.

Though hand in hand the wicked join,
    "They shall be punished," saith the Lord.
Although like floods their strength combined,
    They cannot stay the scourging cord.

For wrongs and outrage shall surcease;
    The millions shall not cry in vain,
For God the captive will release
    And break the bondsman's galling chain.

From 'neath the lash they shall extend
    Their bleeding, trembling hand to God,
And He will to their rescue send
    Stern retribution's chastening rod.

For if the blood of Abel slain
    When crying, reached the Eternal's ear,
And was avenged on guilty Cain,
    Has not this land great cause to fear?

And if the soul poured out in prayer,
    Together with the falling tear,
Be objects of kind Heaven's care,
    Then surely, retribution's near.

And if the darkest hour of night
    Is just before the misty dawn,
Which flies away for morning light,
    To gild and glad the fragrant dawn,

Then soon will freedom's clarion burst,
    In sweet clear strains of liberty,
For of all time this is the worst
    And darkest night of slavery.

When lo! the sages of your land,
　　Assembled in your highest court,
There leagued in sacrilegious band,
　　Send to the world the foul report,

Which herded, with the horse and cow,
　　And merchandise of every name,
All men who wear the sable brow,
　　Regardless of their rank or fame.

"Because the negro's skin is dark,
　　They say, he's made but for a slave;"
They felt not this when he, a mark,
　　On Bunker Hill stood 'mid the brave;

Nor felt they thus when Attucks fell
　　In seventeen seventy—fifth of March.
When proud Boston tolled a bell
　　That caused each freeman's brow to arch.

Attucks, that brave and manly black,
　　Whose heart's blood was the first to flow
When England made her first attack
　　On Boston's freemen, years ago.

Then, then, was that proposal made
　　Which drew those black men in the field,
Who gladly joined the great crusade
　　And learned to die, but not to yield.

They said: "To all who will bear arms,
　　And fight in freedom's holy war,
Will liberty with open arms
　　Receive, and crown with freedom's star."

Then bondmen threw their chains aside,
    And grasped a sword without a sheath,
And to the siege rushed on with pride
    To fight for liberty, or death.

And when old England's ships of war
    Came dashing through the crested foam,
Threatening to blot out every star
    That gemmed and decked their father's home,

Then, black and white men stood abreast,
    A massive wall of living stone,
And on, with earthquake tread, they pressed
    And wrung this land from England's throne.

They, at the siege of Lexington,
    At Bunker Hill and Brandywine,
At Monmouth and at Bennington,
    Marched in freedom's battling line.

Nor did they sheathe their reeking sword,
    Nor lay their heavy armor down,
Till the last booming cannon roared,
    That swept the English from Yorktown.

Black warriors lay amid the host
    That slumbers now near Bunker's heights,
Who fell, contending at their post,
    For liberty and equal rights.

And on every hard-fought field,
    Where freedom's noble sons were slain,
There, stretched beside their battle-shield,
    Lay black and white men on the plain.

When pestilential famine's breath
  Swept through the camp at Valley Forge,
There black and white men slept in death,
  And gentle Schuylkill sang their dirge.

In days of yore, when carnage stared
  This then great nation in the face,
Then blacks, as men they did regard,
  And classed them with the human race.

But now they have no wars to fight,
  No "Independence" to be won;
Sweet, smiling peace veils Bunker's heights,
  And all their battling work is done.

Now from this nation's hall of state
  Comes Roger Tanney's vile decree,
Composed of all the pith and hate
  Of that dark land of slavery.

With him this guilty land unites
  In trampling down the wronged and wrecked,
By claiming Negroes have no rights
  That bind the white man to respect.

And thus the men, whose fathers fought
  Of tyranny this land to rid,
They crushed to earth, without a thought
  Of the great deeds their fathers did.

Alas! are there no meeds of praise
  For freedom's heroes who have died;
Who bore the burden in those days
  When bravest men's brave hearts were tried?

Is gratitude forever dead;
  If not, would they thus destroy
The men, whose fathers fought and bled
  For blessings that they now enjoy?

Look on the face of men like Ward,
  Day, Douglas, Pennington, and then
Tell me whether these should herd
  With beasts of burden or with men.

Why not, in view of all the lights
  That mirror forth the black man's wrongs,
Extend to them those sacred rights
  That justly to a man belongs?

They say he's veiled in sable hues,
  And hence, with them of sinners chief,
They're more fastidious than the Jews,
  Who hung the Christ and spared the thief.

Consistency, spread, spread thy wings!
  Fly! fly! thou hast no mission here;
Fly to the land of pagan kings,
  Unfurl thy bright credentials there.

Thou hast no mission in a land
  Where man is crushed for being black;
As well go preach among the damned,
  Or sing songs to a maniac.

But, oh, how long, great God! how long
  Shall this sad state of things remain;
How long shall right succumb to wrong;
  How long shall justice plead in vain?

How long! Oh, may we live to see
  That natal day of jubilee,
When every fetter shall be riven,
  And every heart praise God in heaven.

————

The Dawn of Freedom.*

When summer's hot and sultry rays
  Are burdening our summer days,
  And men and beast are sore oppress'd,
  And vainly sigh and pant for rest;
  Rest from the turbid cares of life,
Their wild convulsions and its strife—
Then something whispers in our ear,
And tells us of a covert near;
A quiet, soft and cool retreat,
Where morn and evening dew drops meet;
Where Nature, in her gorgeous dress,
Stands forth in all her loveliness;
And where the gentle zephyrs play,
And sport with leaflets all the day.

————

*Delivered at River Park, Toledo, August 3, 1868,
at the grand festival in commemoration of the abolition
of slavery in the British West India Isles.

Oh! who would not for such a scene
Of artless beauty, native sheen,
Turn from the busy haunts of men,
And from the city's noxious fen,
And hie to some sequestered nook,
Some peaceful dell beside the brook,
Or bask within the ample shade
Of some proud monarch of the glade,
Where every passing breath of air,
Comes fraught with odors rich and rare;
Though housed beneath this sylvan bower,
Where Sol's hot rays lose half their power,
And where the green sward at our feet,
Invites us to an humble seat,
Yet come we not from homes afar,
By coach and boat and flying car,
These native scenes to eulogize,
How much soe'er their wealth we prize.
'Tis not of thee my native land,
     Nor of thy triple folds so bright,
Nor of thy legions proud and grand,
     That slew oppression in the fight.
'Tis not of thee, though worthy thou
Of many a song and plighted vow.
'Tis not of thee that we have ta'en,
Our *harp* to wake its humble strain;
But of a land and far away,
     Bathed by the ever restless sea;
A land where freedom's sons to-day,
     Are met in gladsome jubilee.
With them we would commemorate
     An epoch in the march of years,
An epoch ever proud and great,
     The chief of freedom's pioneers.
A day that saw a million chains
     Fall from a million shackled limbs,

And heard a million glad refrains,
  Of mingled shouts and prayers and hymns.
A day that saw a million men
  Stand up in God's pure sunlight free,
Who never in all their lives till then,
  Had breathed one breath of liberty.
The driver's horn, at early morn,
  Had bid them to their task repair,
Where oft the lash, and many a gash
  Was waiting their arrival there.
And thus they had from youth to age,
  And from the cradle to the tomb,
Been driven forth from stage to stage,
  Through moral night and mental gloom.
The day that saw their fetters riven;
  The day that saw their gloom depart,
And heard their prayers and thank-shouts given
  To freedom's God, fresh from the heart.
They've met to-day to celebrate,
  And while they sing our songs shall rise,
And bowing, we shall venerate
  A common parent in the skies.
Hail! hail! glad day, thy blest return,
  We greet with prayer and speech and song,
And while from eulogies full urn,
  We drink to thee, march proudly on.
March proudly on as heretofore,
  Thou Black man's borrowed day of joy,
For long our native land was poor,
  Too poor to yield such grand employ;
Columbia had her many days
  Of frolic, sport and joy, and glee;
But none of universal praise;
  No soul-inspiring jubilee;
No day on which, from palace dome
  And from the lowly thatched-roof tent,

Would mutual heartfelt greetings come,
    Memorial of some grand event.
She had her Independence day,
    But what was July's Fourth to him
Whose class and kind and kindred lay,
    All fetter-bound in mind and limb;
And what the pilgrim's yearly feast,
    And what the birth of Washington,
To him whose grievous bonds increased
    With each new day's unfolding sun?
He had no day—there was not one
    Of all the days that formed the year,
Which did not point to wrongs begun,
    And oft beguile him of a tear.
And thus ten score of years passed by,
    And yet no star of hope arose—
No rainbow arched his gloomy sky,
    Nor respite offered to his woes.
Hence, when at length the British Isles,
    Burst forth in shouts of liberty,
He set at naught a thousand miles,
    And joined them in their jubilee.
Glad but to know on God's green *earth,*
    One spot was consecrate and free,
Where *Truth* and right had given birth
    Unto a black man's jubilee!
Though subjects of another land,
    And dwellers 'mid a tropic sea,
Yet they, like him, had worn the brand,
    And now were what he longed to be.
And in that act he faintly scan'd
    The outstretched arms of Deity;
Extending t'ward his native land,
    The golden wand of Liberty,
And dimly saw four million chains,
    In broken wild disorder lay.

And Slavery's blight with all its stains,
  Banished his native land for aye—
Hence, when upon the wheels of time,
  The glorious First would roll its round,
His gladsome notes with theirs would chime,
  And cause the valleys to resound—
In honor of that day and deed
When Briton's swarthy sons were freed—
That day when Justice wrenched from Might
  The keys of power so long detained,
And clothed on man his every right,
  Which foul oppression had restrained.
That day, when, after twenty years'
  Persistence, pleading and appeal,
Midst all the scorn and taunt and jeers
  That selfish bigots dare reveal—
When those who pleaded had grown gray,
And many, alas! had passed away—
Passed away, and left undone
The work their noble hearts begun.
But Wilberforce—long live his name!
With trembling voice, still pressed his claim
In Parliament, in Court, or Hall;
His theme was, LIBERTY FOR ALL!
He claimed that Briton had no right
To suffer man, nor black nor white,
To wear perforce a slavish chain
Within her realm, by land or main,
That such too long had been the case.
And even then, to her disgrace,
A group of Isles, far out from land,
And sheltering 'neath her own command,
Were pouring forth a piteous wail
On every breeze and passing gale.
His voice at length Britannia heard,
And lo! her mighty heart was stirred—

Stirred for the tale so often told,
And unto thousands had grown old,
Fell for the first time on her ear,
And from her heart compelled a tear—
Compelled a tear for the man enchained—
Compelled a tear for the sin which stained
The proud escutcheon of her land,
And stamped it with a slaver's brand.
Then swiftly went an edict forth,
Of grave importance, matchless worth;
Close followed by that proud decree
Which swept the land and swept the sea,
Where'er the British flag unfurled
Throughout the regions of the world,
And there established in the name
Of Briton's throne, of Britain's fame,
Upon the purest, broadest plan,
ETERNAL LIBERTY FOR MAN!
Then Freedom's joyous angel flew
    With lightning speed o'er land and wave,
And loud her clarion trumpet blew,
    And woke to life each panting slave.
Woke them to life? They did not sleep,
    But there in anxious silence stood,
Waiting the welcome sound to sweep
    Athwart Atlantic's briny flood.
And when the sound fell on their ear,
They laughed, they wept, they knelt in prayer;
And rising from their bended knees,
They sang in joyous ecstacies,
Till hill and vale and distant plain
Gave back the gladsome sound again.
Oh! for a Raphael's hand to draw
    The matchless grandeur of that sight,
That earth might see as angels saw
    From off the parapets of light;

For shining ones of heavenly birth
 Bent o'er the jasper walls on high,
And caught the jubilant songs of earth,
 And bore them upward to the sky;
And Heaven gave audience to the strain
 Of those fair minstrels as they sang,
Gathering up the glad refrain
 With which the hills and valleys rang,
And sending them forever on,
 And on, and on, eternally;
For Heaven itself can boast no song
 Of sweeter strain than Liberty.
The heart with exultation glows,
 Discanting on the joyous theme
Of broken chains and buried woes—
 'Twere glorious, though 'twere but a dream.
But since it is a truth sublime,
 On history's page inscribed as such,
And brightening with the march of time,
 We cannot say in praise too much.
We cannot laud the truth too high,
 Nor praise too much the noble deed;
Nor can we brand too deep the lie
 Where innocence is caused to bleed;
Nor can we say too much in praise
 Of Britain's *bloodless victory;*
Nor of the glow and halo blaze
 Which circled INDIA'S JUBILEE,
When Freedom waved her wand and spoke,
And lo! a million chains were broke.
No weary interregnum lay
'Twixt Slavery's night and Freedom's day;
But when their fetters fell to earth,
'Twas followed by a very birth.
And in the change which there began,
Stood up a Briton and a man—

A Briton, in fact, in every sense,
His new creation to commence.
Though great as was this noble deed,
Whereby a million souls were freed,
And a million Britons made
Of men, whom crime had long betrayed.
Yet 'twas no action based upon
Some worthy deed these may have done—
Some service rendered in a time
Of revolution, blood and crime.
No, these had no such claims to press—
Their only plea was their distress;
They ne'er had fought 'gainst Scot or Dane,
That British freedom might obtain;
Nor had they in dread peril's hour,
When bravest hearts were wont to cower,
Been called to take a *patriot's* stand
And quell the treason of the land.
Yet, when their liberties were given
'Twas like the genial rays of heaven—
So pure, so just—no rights denied;
'Twas Freedom, broad, unqualified.
Yes, Freedom in its broadest sense,
Of unrestrained significance;
No force work that—no soulless cheat;
But thorough, once done and complete!
In this, Britannia's proudest act,
The world beheld a noble fact;
They saw what truth had long required—
Humanity had long desired—
They saw it, and they understood,
For Britain did it as she should;
She broke the yoke, banished the chain,
And left no link thereof remain!
No, not in all her broad spread land
Left she a relic of the brand!

But let us here a question press:
Could she, in justice, have done less;
Could she a single right suppress
And not have made a mockery
Of all her towers of Liberty?
Would not the whole, from base to dome,
Become the meanest cheat, a sham, a gnome
Whereon the finger of disdain
Might trace the link-marks of the chain?
Though men may prate of Blacks and Whites,
There is no such thing as halving rights!
All partial justice is unjust,
And merits man's profound distrust!
In truth there is no safety short
Of freedom's unrestrained resort;
All less than this is tyranny—
All more than that is bigotry.
The principle, that dare withold
The least known rights, on growing bold,
Would grind the subject to a brute
And e'en the claim to life dispute,
Despite all vain prerogatives!
Despite the fame which power gives —
Despite the verdict of the throng.
What e'er curtails a right is wrong
And quite as wrong in temperate zone
    As 'twere beneath a tropic sky;
'Neath a Republic or a Throne
    'Twere but the same, a heartless lie!
'Gainst which in Truth all conquering might
The brave should arm themselves and fight
For manhood, self-hood and the right,
Valiant and fearless, though all alone,
Knowing that if they battle on,
That in the future ever near
To those who fight, and trust and fear,

Success will crown their work of love,
And God, in smiling from above,
Will say, *"Well done, faithful and true,*
A crown of stars and a robe's thy due!"
Now cast your eyes o'er this fair land,
    Where hopes and fears alternate rise,
Where long the demon of the brand
    Stalked boldly forth in native guise.
Here, where in opulence he sat,
    And waved his ebon rod of might,
And waved it where our rulers met,
    And many trembled at the sight,
Their trembling fed his arrogance
    And flattered his ambitious dream,
Till puffed with vain intolerance,
    He dared aspire to rule supreme,
And seized the dictatorial chair—
    Blandished the weapons of his power,
And by his own vain greatness swore
    To rule or ruin from that hour.
Then rose the legions of the North
    In all their majesty and might,
And 'gainst his minions and the South
    Went forth to battle and to fight;
And after much of wasted life,
    Attended by a fearful cost,
The South, o'ercome, gave up the strife,
    And all her hopes as staked and lost.
Had then this land her duty done,
    In justice and without delay,
There would have been beneath the sun
    No land so free as this today.
Not only would the chain be broke,
    But veil be rent and wall removed,
And all that would the taunt provoke
    In simple justice disapprove

All the base relics of the night,
  Of barbarism's foulsome reign;
We should have banished at the sight
  Of reason's torch and freedom's train,
For there's no spot where in its pride
  Yon tri-hued starry flag doth wave,
That manhood's claims should be denied,
  Or rights withheld the recent slave.
The yester bondsman must be made
  Not only part, but wholly free:
There must not live a single shade
  To dim his manhood's *liberty;*
When such obtains, throughout the land,
  Then shall this gladsome song be sung
By myriad voices proud and grand,
  The aged mingling with the young:
"The long black night of bondage,
  With all its fiendish train,
Of nameless wrongs and outrage,
  At length has ceased to reign;
And Freedom has arisen,
  And gone forth in her might,
Nor left a slavish prison
  Her glorious name to blight;
And chains that were enthralling,
  The friendless and the poor,
And yokes that were so galling,
  Have changed to molten ore;
And o'er our mighty nation,
  Now and forever free,
Floats proud in exultation,
  Our Bird of Liberty.
Throw out your starry banners,
  And let them float the gale,
Sweeping our broad Savannas,
  With freedom in their trail—

Out, out! on every flag-staff,
  Or low or towering grand,
Out and let the welkin laugh
  In honor of our land;
And you, ye lofty mountains,
  And gorgeous vales profound,
Where gush forth crystal fountains,
  Your gladsome notes resound;
And lake and flowing river,
  And streamlets everywhere,
In ripling wavelets quiver
  The joys ye would declare;
And merry woodland songsters,
  And beast and lowing kine,
And fish and ocean monster
  Your varied notes combine—
Then shall the sons of gladness,
  Five millions, wronged, arise,
And with the shouts of gladness
  All nature vocalize,
Until the hosts of Heaven
  Shall catch the joyous strain,
Floating aloft unriven,
  From mountain, vale and main;
And by that crystal river,
  And on that glassy sea,
Where harpers stand forever,
  Reecho Liberty;
For O, there is in earth or Heaven
  No sweeter note or purer key
To mortals known, or angels given,
  Than peerless, chainless LIBERTY!"
Now in conclusion e'er we lay
  Our shattered harp in silence by,
  To westward turn the mental eye,
And once more greet the far away.

Though years have passed since freedom's morn,
  First dawned on those glad Isles at sea,
Yet there to-day is upward borne,
  The grateful peans of the free—
To God, who holds within his hands
The destiny of men and lands;
The destiny of every sphere
In heaven's blue fields remote or near—
To Him, God of the earth and skies,
To-day their songs and prayers arise.
And thus we stretch our puny arm,
  Across the broad, unfathomed deep,
With heart-congratulations warm,
  For all the free-born joys they reap.
Long may their Island-home remain,
  As now, beneath the fostering care
Of Freedom's wise and glorious reign,
  Where each his manly rights may share.
Long may the banner of the free,
Wave o'er them in its purity—
Pure as the zephyrs in their flight—
Chaste as the radiant stars of night.

Introductory Note.

The Poet laments the discord of his Harp, and its disuse, until answering Freedom's call he again essays its harmony. He portrays the conflict, and gives thanks to God for the dawning day of Freedom. He rejoices that Columbia is free; he eulogizes the moral heroes, and describes how America is "marching on" in the footsteps of the warlike "Hero John."

The cause of this fratricidal war is next given, and the challenge of Slavery to Liberty. He then invokes the spirits of our "sleeping sires" from their "beds of dust," and bids the nation listen to their warning voices. He concludes by prophecying that a glorious peace will be secured when Liberty is inscribed upon the banners of the Union.

Emancipation of the slaves in the District of Columbia and in the British West Indies.

Harp of my soul, though thou hast hung
    Suspended from the willow bough
    Till much distorted, warped and sprung,
    And discord reigns within thee now,
    Yet glad I take thee thence again,
Responsive to the joyous call,
Which comes from isles far o'er the main,
And from this nation's stately hall.

Thy shattered chords I strive to mend,
    That they may no preventive be.
And all thy latent powers I'll bend
    To chant one song to Liberty.
O, Liberty! inspiring theme,
Thou innate boon from God to man!
Without thee joy were but a dream,
    And life—a drear and wretched span.

But with thee, every breeze that's given
    Seems wafted from some sunny isle;
They swell the heart with joyous leaven,
    And paint the cheek with pleasure's smile.
Oh! heavenly boon, destined to be
    This erring nation's honored guest,
When shall the blessings of the free
    Pervade the millions now oppressed?

Hark, hark! what sounds are those that sweep
Thitherward o'er the vasty deep?
Louder by far than aught before—
Terrible as the thunder's roar!
Lo! 'tis the clash of Freedom's stars
Rushing on to the field of Mars;
Rushing on with a force unknown—
Rushing on through the torrid zone;

Legion's their name, and in their wake
The heavens veil and the mountains quake,
And streamlets, long before run dry,
Now flood the land with crimson dye,
While 'long their banks, o'er field and plain,
Are thickly strewn the recent slain,
And from the breath, which they exhale,
A rank miasma fills the vale.

Thank God! a glorious dawn betides
    Oppression's long and rayless night,
And one that promise well provides
    With many a hoped for ray of light—
A light that bids far to extend,
    E'en to the deepest, darkest vales,
And from visual orbits rend
    All vile accumulated scales.

For Liberty, though long enthralled,
    Is rending now each servile band,
And will, ere long, become installed
    Proud monarch of this glorious land;
The tiny cloud, the promise star,
    Are now above the horizon—
Behold them, through the ranks of war,
    In graceful triumph marching on.

Unfurl your banners to the breeze—
　Let Freedom's tocsin sound amain!
Until the islands of the seas
　Re-echo with the glad refrain:
Columbia's free! Columbia's free!
　Her teeming streets, her vine-clad groves,
Are sacred now to Liberty
　And God, where every right approves.

Thank God, the Capital is free;
　The slaver's pen, the auction block,
And gory lash of cruelty
　No more this nation's pride shall mock;
No more within those ten miles square
　Shall men be bought and women sold,
Or infants sable-hued and fair,
　Exchanged again for paltry gold.

Today the Capital is free!
　And free those halls where Adams stood
And plead for man's humanity,
　And for a common brotherhood;
Where Sumner stood, whose world wide fame
　And eloquent philosophy
Has clustered, round his deathless name,
　Bright laurels for eternity;

Where Wilson, Lovejoy, Wade and Hale,
　And other lights of equal power,
Have stood, like warriors clad in mail,
　Before the giant of this hour,
Co-workers in a common cause,
　Laboring for their country's weal
By just enactments, righteous laws,
　And burning, eloquent appeal;

To whom we owe, and gladly bring,
    The grateful tributes of our hearts.
And while we live to muse and sing,
    These in our songs shall claim their parts.
For now Columbia's air doth seem
    Much purer than in days agone,
And now her mighty heart, I deem,
    Has lighter grown by marching on!

Marching on! through blood and strife,
Marching on! through wasted life,
Marching on! to the glorious day
When the last foul brand is swept away.
Marching on! o'er the graveless dead,
Marching on! through streamlets red—
Red with the vain hearts ebbing tide
Of rebels slain in their vaunted pride.

Marching on! with a foot as firm
As that which careless treads the worm,
With sword unsheathed and power to wield,
And a dauntless heart that will not yield.
Thus Liberty goes marching on,
Step for step, with the "hero John!"
In whom oppression basely slew
The bravest son e'er freedom knew.

He fell—but Freedom set her price,
Counting his silver threads o'er thrice;
She pledged to each and every one
A heartless tyrant sire or son,
But while her lenient wrath delayed,
Still fiercer grew oppression's raid,
And when denied the Chair of State,
He boldly donned the guise of hate.

And forthwith armed his minions all,
With rifle, cannon, bomb and ball,
And in the frenzy of his ire,
On Sumpter rained a storm of fire.
Thus slavery threw the gauntlet down,
And stripped it bare of every guise,
Then rent a star from Freedom's crown
And closed the door of compromise.

Though Liberty indignant grew,
  Yet, with an all-forbearing hand,
She strove to tame the ranting shrew,
  And save the glory of her land.
But no! a tyrant's cup of guilt
  Was now preparing to run o'er —
The sheathless sword, from point to hilt,
  Must revel in the purple gore.

From warnings oft they'd nothing learned,
  In sin more sinful still had grown,
Till Heaven's displeasure they have earned,
  And lo! their blood must now atone.
Warned by all their sleeping sires,
  Whose lives were pledged 'gainst tyranny,
Who taught, beside their homestead fires,
  The dread results of slavery;

Who drew from reason living facts,
  Based on the ever present past,
To prove that sure destruction tracks
  Oppression's train, however vast,
And floating down the lapse of years,
  Their voice of warning calls to us,
In tones expressive of their fears—
  Fears for their country's future—thus:

"We find within the Book of Fate
    This page of small uncertainty:
At any risk, however great,
    Ere long the bondmen will be free:
For when the measure of their grief
    Will not contain another tear,
And bitter groanings call relief,
    Then surely God will interfere.

"Beware, lest what ye deal to those,
    At length upon yourselves recoil—
The arm of right will interpose,
    And then the spoiled will reap the spoil.
For wrong doth execute with wrong,
    And surely will he execute,
Though retributions tarry long—
    Yet fail they never in their fruit.

"When we the future contemplate,
    And then reflect that God is just,
We tremble for our country's fate."
    Thus speak they from their beds of dust.
Nor could they, even had the cloud
    Which veils the future from our view
Been quite removed, and they allowed
    To range beyond, spoke aught more true.

What if the dead, the noble dead,
    Keep watch above their former state;
Would these no spirit-tears have shed
    O'er scenes enacted here of late?
Think you that shriek and dying groan
    Arising from the gory sward,
Could sweep athwart their spirit zone
    And stir no sympathetic chord?

But wherefore this unmeaning strife,
And wherefore all this waste of life?
The richest blood of northern veins
Is pouring out like heaven's rains;
And still their braves are rallying round
The stripes and stars, at the bugle sound;
But still we press the question, why
Are all these brave ones called to die?

Why, is the bristling bayonet
Upon the death charged rifle set?
Why does the deafening cannon's roar,
Reverberate from shore to shore?
And why (the question still is pressed),
Why is the nation sore distressed?

America! America!
    Thine own undoing thou hast wrought,
For all thy wrongs to Africa
    This cup has fallen to thy lot,
Whose dregs of bitterness shall last
    Till thou acknowledge God in man;
Till thou undo thine iron grasp,
    And free thy brother and his clan.

Till thou restore again the pledge,
The garment, and the golden wedge;
Till Achan, and his latest kin,
Without the camp shall meet their sin.
Till then, this fratricidal war,
Which all so justly should abhor,
Will neither change its wasting mood,
Nor with a shallow truce conclude.

No! no! there ne'er will come a peace,
Nor will this war of brothers cease,
While on Columbia's fair domain,
A single bondsman clanks his chain.
For God, who works through fire and sword,
And through the spirit of His word,
Has witnessed all their bitter grief,
And now has come to their relief.

Tó hasten freedom's glorious time,
    And save in treasure and in life,
Count Hunter's policy no crime;
    Arm each and all to end the strife.
Upon your rallying banner's write,
    The magic words of liberty—
And thousands, panting for the fight,
    Will press to war and victory.

Then will the Northern loyal blacks,
    Who anxious are to join the fray,
Soon buckle on their haversacks,
    And shoulder arms, and hie away.
And then the war which bids to last
Through years to come, will soon be past
And rolling years shall but increase
In permanence our glorious peace.

For the land shall bloom when the foe is slain,
And peace, long exiled, shall return again;
And the door of Janus again shall close,
And the crimson's sword in its sheath repose;
And the galling chain, and yoke of the slave,
Shall pollute no more the home of the brave.
Till then let us pray—till then let us trust
Ever in God, who is faithful and just.

CAPT. JOHN BROWN
OF HARPERS' FERRY FAME

THE DAY AND THE WAR.

SACRED TO THE MEMORY OF THE IMMORTAL

CAPTAIN JOHN BROWN,

THE HERO, SAINT AND MARTYR OF HARPER'S FERRY,

The following poem is most respectfully inscribed,
by one who loved him in life, and in death
would honor his memory.

Introductory Note.

The Poet laments the long years of enslave-
ment of his race, but rejoices that the Emancipa-
tion Proclamation is the harbinger of the good
time coming, and has at length given him

"A fitting day to celebrate."

He shows how this wicked Rebellion, instituted
to perpetuate Slavery, will cause "the final aboli-
tion" of the accursed institution.—The Colored

people are incited to prove themselves worthy of
the position they must assume, by patriotism, for-
titude and virtue.

The deceitful policy of the European Govern-
ments is examined and criticised—their jealousy
of the growing power of the American Union;
their sympathy with the Rebels; the material aid
and comfort they render unto the Confederacy,
and their desire to effect the dismemberment of
the Republic. England, remembering the loss of
the Colonies, is covertly aiding the Rebellion, and,
while professing neutrality, is supplying them
with ships and munitions of war.

He next sings of the heroism of the colored
troops—their deeds of valor at Milliken's Bend—
bravery of Miller's men, of which company all
save one were either slain or wounded—and of
the heroic achievements of the Black Brigade.

He relates a vision of the War, and portrays
in vivid colors the horrors of a battlefield after
the fight. An angel appears, who announces the
advent of Peace. The warrior returns from the
carnage of battle; his sword is turned into a plow-
share, his spear into a reaping-hook, and a "real
Republic" is formed.

In conclusion, he eulogizes the God-approving
act of President Lincoln in issuing the great
Emancipation Proclamation, and predicts that
when posterity is enumerating the benefactors of
mankind, "great Lincoln's name will lead the
host."

                                   P. A. BELL.

The Day and The War.

Twelve score of years were long to wait
A fitting day to celebrate:
'Twere long upon one's native soil
A feeless drudge in pain to toil.
But Time that fashions and destroys,
And breeds our sorrows, breeds our joys,
Hence we at length have come with cheer,
To greet the dawning of the year—
The bless'd return of that glad day,
When, through Oppression's gloom, a ray
Of joy and hope and freedom burst,
Dispelling that insatiate thirst,
Which anxious years of toil and strife
Had mingled with the bondman's life.

A fitting day for such a deed,
But far more fit, when it shall lead
To the final abolition
Of the last slave's sad condition;
Then, when the New Year ushers in,
A grand rejoicing shall begin;
Then shall Freedom's clarion tone
Arouse no special class alone,
But all the land its blast shall hear,
And hail with joy the jubilant year;
And maid and matron, youth and age,
Shall meet upon one common stage,
And Proclamation Day shall be
A National Day of Jubilee.

No longer 'neath the weight of years—
No longer merged in hopeless fears—
Is now that good time, long delayed,
When right, not might, shall all pervade.
Drive hence despair—no longer doubt,
Since friends within and foes without
Their might and main conjointly blend
To reach the same great, glorious end—
The sweeping from this favored land
The last foul chain and slavish brand.

No longer need the bondman fear,
For lo! the good time 's almost here,
And doubtless some beneath our voice
Shall live to hail it and rejoice;
For almost now the radiant sheen
Of freedom's glad hosts may be seen;
The ear can almost catch the sound,
The eye can almost see them bound,
As thirty million voices rise
In grateful peans to the skies.

But of the present we would sing,
    And of a land all bathed in blood—
A land where plumes the eagle's wing,
    Whose flaming banner, stars bestud—
A land where Heaven, with bounteous hand,
    Rich gifts hath strewn for mortal weal,
Till vale and plain and mountain grand
    Have each a treasure to reveal:
A land with every varying clime,
    From torrid heat to frigid cold—
With natural scenery more sublime
    Than all the world beside unfold,
Where vine-clad France may find a peer,
    And Venice an Italian sky,

With streams whereon the gondolier
 His feather'd oar with joy may ply.
O, heaven-blest and favored land,
 Why are thy fruitful fields laid waste?
Why with thy fratricidal hand
 Hast thou thy beauty half defaced?
Why do the gods disdain thy prayer?
 And why in thy deep bitterness
Comes forth no heaven-clothed arm to share
 A part, and help in the distress?

Hast thou gone forth to reap at noon
And gather where thou hadst not strewn
Hast thou kept back the hireling's fee,
And mocked him in his poverty?
Hast thou, because thy God hath made
Thy brother of a different shade,
Bound fast the iron on his limb,
And made a feeless drudge of him?
Hast thou, to fill thy purse with gold,
The offsprings of his nature sold?
And in thy brutal lust, beguiled
His daughter and his couch defiled?

 For all this wrong and sad abuse,
Hast thou no offering of excuse?
No plea to urge in thy defense
'Gainst helpless, outraged innocence?
Then fearful is thy doom indeed,
If guilty thou canst only plead.
Thy sin is dark, and from the law
No dint of pity canst thou draw.
If thou are charged, 'twill hear thy suit;
If guilty, swift to execute,
Eye for an eye and tooth for tooth;
Yet, Oh forbid it, God of truth:

Let not thine arm in anger fall,
But hear a guilty nation's call;
And stay the vial of wrath at hand,
Pour not its contents on the land;
Should they the last dregs in the cup
Of bitterness be called to sup,
And all the contents of the vial
Of thy just wrath be poured the while,
With all the tortures in reserve,
'Twould scarce be more than they deserve,
For they have sinned 'gainst thee and man.
But wilt thou not, by thy own plan,
Bring them past this sea of blood,
Ere they are buried 'neath its flood?

America! I thee conjure,
By all that's holy, just and pure,
To cleanse thy hands from Slavery's stain,
And banish from thy soil the chain.
Thou canst not thrive, while with the sweat
Of unpaid toil thy lands are wet,
Nor canst thou hope for peace or joy
Till thou Oppression doth destroy.

Already in the tented field
Are thy proud hosts that will not yield—
Already are they sweeping forth,
Like mighty whirlwinds from the North,
And from the East and West afar
With earthquake tread they press to war,
Until, from where Atlantic raves,
And wildly beats his rock-bound shore,
To where the calm Pacific laves
A land of fruits and shining oar,
The thundering voice of Mars is heard,
And echoing vales repeat each word,

And mountains tremble to their base!
For lo! in arms a mighty race,
Of mighty genius, mighty strength,
Have ta'en the field as foes at length,—
A nation, whom but yesterday
The bands of union joined in one,
Now clad in war's dread panoply,
Their marshaling hosts to battle run.
But not as blind ambition's slaves
Rush wildly on those breathing waves:
Nor as the dread sirocco's breath,
All indiscriminate in death—
But they (as freemen should and must,
When ruthless, ruffian hands assail
Their rightful cause of sacred trust,
And 'gainst that cause would fain prevail),
Have seized the rifle, sword and spear,
And charged upon the foeman near.

And Europe's clans all interest grew,
When North and South their sabres drew,
For they had long with jealous fear
Marked this vast Republic here,
And watched its almost magic growth,
Compared with their dull rounds of sloth;
Hence, when the bomb on Sumter fell,
They felt a half-unconscious swell
Of exultation flame the heart,
And only hoped, that bomb might part
The web and woof which bound in one
Their greatest rival 'neath the sun.
For where's the monarch that could rest
Secure beneath his royal crest,
And see a land like this of ours—
Radiant with eternal flowers,
With hills and vales of solid gold,

That centuries yet will scarce unfold,
And holding out a welcome hand
To all the subjects of his land,
And they responding to the call
Like the sear'd foliage of the fall—
And feel no inward joy or pride
In aught that promised to divide,
And e'en to tatter'd fragments rend,
The land where all those virtues blend?
For scarce a wave that sweeps the sea,
However small or great it be,
Nor scarce a sail that drinks the spray,
But bears some despot's slave away.

Hence to the North their word of mouth,
While heart and soul's been with the South—
Been with the South from first to last,
And will be till the war is past,
Despite non-intervention's cry,—
Which, by-the-way, a blacker lie
Ne'er came from Pandemonium's cell
Nor from the foulest niche in hell,
Than 'twere for Europe to affirm
    That she has wholly neutral kept,
The while this dark and fearful storm
    Of civil war has o'er us swept;
Not intervene, and still erect
    Rebel warships by the score,
And give them succor, and protect
    Upon her coast as many more?
Not intervene! Whence the supply
    Of war munitions by the ton,
That sweep our blocking squadrons by,
    And into Southern harbors run?
Not intervene, and 'neath her dock
    Shelter a well-known privateer—

And to prevent her capture, mock
With self-raised queries till she's clear?
Not intervene! and yet propose
To recognize the South when she
Discards the source of half her woes,
And sets her long bound captives free?
If this non-intervention is,
Then O may Jeff deliver us:
For better had we bow as his,
Than fall where nations reason thus.

All this was done, but wonder not
The half-healed wound is ne'er forgot;
It may assume perfection's state
And e'en the heart with joy elate;
While crouched beneath a gauze-like crest,
Its germ and root and fibres rest;
Where slightest scratch or bruise or sprain
May wake them into life again.

Thus Britain wounded years before,
Remembers still the painful sore,
And were the time more opportune,
Columbia's sun she'd veil at noon.
She's envious of her growing wealth,
Her fruitful fields, her joy, her health,
Her mighty rivers grand and free,
Creation's highways to the sea:
And fain would sway her sceptred hand,
And bring them all 'neath her command;
For kindred spirits there are none,
Twixt a Republic and a throne.

Then wonder not that Europe's choice,
Her strength of purse, her strength of voice,
Have favored every foul excess

Through which this nation might grow less.
And that this wasting war proceed,
And to the utter ruin lead
Of this Republic, they have prayed,
And praying lent the South their aid;
And hence the war is raging still,
And the nation's good or ill
Hangs on the issue of the fight—
The triumph of the wrong or right.

Many have been the grounds of strife
Where man has sacrificed his life,
And many causeless wars have been
Since Michael fought and conquered sin;
Yet many battles have been fought,
And many lands that blood have bought,
Through wars that have been justified,
Where struggling thousands fought and died—
Fought and died, and were proud that they
On the shrine of truth had a life to lay;
Fought and died, nor trembling came
They to the life-devouring flame,
But, like Winkleride of yore,
Their sheathless breasts they bravely bore.

For he who battles for the right,
When in the thickest of the fight,
Doth feel a God-approving glow,
Which bids defiance to the foe;
And though he falls beside his shield,
He sleeps a victor on the field.
And Freedom is that sacred cause,
    Where he that doth his lancet poise,
Shall, living, reap the world's applause,
    Or, dying, win unclouded joys.

But now the query to be solved
Is, shall the Union be dissolved?
Shall this fair land, our fathers gave
Ungrudgingly their lives to save
From kingly rule and tyranny,
Be rent in twain by Slavery?
And shall the line of Plymouth stock—
Whose sires trod that hoary rock,
Which rendered sacred e'en the soil
Whereon they after deign'd to toil—
Allow this refuge of black lies,
Quintessence of all villanies,
To rear thereon his demon throne,
Or claim one footprint as his own?

What, though the dark and foulsome raid
Of South Carolina should pervade
The whole entire South, and they,
Like hungry wolves in quest of prey,
Rush down upon the Union fold,
Rivaling e'en the Gauls of old?
Shall we, because of that dark raid,
See Freedom's shrine in ruins laid,
And her long-spread banner furl'd,
To grow the butt of all the world:
And passive keep, the while this horde,
From mountain height and valley pour'd,
Ride rampant over field and plain,
Dread carnage strewing in their train,
Until they plant their standard, where
Old Bunker rears his head in air?

To gain this zenith of their pride,
Through human gore waste-deep they'd ride.
Waist-deep! aye, more—they love the sin,
And some would brave it to the chin,

Could they upon old Bunker's mound
Dole out their man flesh by the pound!
Nor would they with their souls demur,
E'en though the venal purchaser
Should in his fiendish lust demand
The fairest daughters of the land;
Nor would they scruple as to hue,
But eyes of jet and eyes of blue,
And fair-brow'd maids with flowing hair,
Such as Anglo-Saxons wear,
Would grace as oft their auction-blocks
As those less fair with fleecy locks.

But never! never! never, no!
No, never while the North winds blow,
Shall vile oppression desecrate
One foot of earth in that old State!
Not while the gallant Fifty-fourth,
In all the spirit of the North,
Stand pledged Secession to defy,
Or in the cause of Freedom die;
Not while a single hand remains
To grasp the sword or touch the spring,
Shall that foul dagon god of chains
Thither his courts and altars bring.

To this audacious end they've bent
    Their ever-craven, vulturous eye,
Till now their fiendish, dark intent,
    Stands out before the noonday sky;
And all equip'd for death and war,
With rifle, bomb and cimeter,
They boldly stand on Richmond's height,
And claim secession as a right.
But, whether right or wrong, still they
Have sworn no longer to obey

Edict sent or mandate given,
From any court this side of Heaven,
Except that court in concert be
With chains and endless slavery.

At length the war assumes a phase,
    Though long apparent, oft denied:
We speak it in the nation's praise—
    The land they never can divide.
Therefore this fact should none surprise—
If Slavery lives, the Union dies;
And if the Union's e'er restored,
'Twill be when Freedom is secured;
And liberty, man's rightful due,
Is not proscribed by grade nor hue.
Hence he that would avert the doom,
And rescue from sepulchral gloom
His freedom, must, with sword in hand,
March 'gainst the slavery of this land.

    Then gird thy loins, for lo! thy course,
O brother! long oppress'd by force,
With stalwart arm and ebon brow,
Was never half so plain as now:
Nor half so ominously bright
With Hope's refulgent beams of light—
For with each deafening cannon's roar,
Thy hated chains grow less secure:
And, like the fumes of war, shall they
Dissolve ere long, and pass away.
Meanwhile, from thraldom's gloomy slough
Millions shall come forth such as thou,
And Fame a laurel wreath shall twine
For many a brow of Afric line.

But prate thou not of liberty,
While still in shackled slavery
The most remote of all thy kin
Bow down beneath its damning sin!
Nor make thy boast of English birth,
Nor French descent, nor Celtic worth;
This leave for English, French or Dane,
Whose kindred wear no galling chain.
But thou, O man of Afric hue,
This vaunting spirit pray subdue,
And bide thy time to boast till he,
Thy last chained brother, shall be free.

Not only free from lash and yoke,
But free from all that should provoke
The just, indignant wrath of those
Who now his budding rights oppose;
Not only free to shoulder arms,
When foeman thick as locusts swarm,
Securely wrapped in coats of mail,
Seem almost certain to prevail;
Not only free to pay a tax
To each scrip-monger, who exacts
His hard-earned dollar as a rule,
For purposes of State or school:
While they the children of his loins,
Through some base act which hate enjoins,
Are not allowed within the door
Where Wisdom sits to bless the poor!
Not only free to tell the truth
Where Justice, mocked at, sits forsooth!
But free from all that should impair
The rights of freemen anywhere!

Till then, thou shouldst not, must not boast,
But rather at thy lowly post,

With zeal and fortitude combined,
Discharge the duties there assigned.
Should struggling Freedom call for thee,
Come forth with proud alacrity;
Gird on dread war's habiliments,
And nobly stand in her defense,
And thereby thou shalt win a place
For thee and for thy injured race,
Above the vulgar taunt and jeer,
That grates so harshly on thy ear.

———

THOUGH Tennyson, the poet king,
    Has sung of Balaklava's charge,
Until his thund'ring cannons ring
    From England's center to her marge,
The pleasing duty still remains
To sing a people from their chains—
To sing what none have yet assay'd,
The wonders of the Black Brigade.
The war had raged some twenty moons,
Ere they in columns or platoons,
To win them censure or applause,
Were marshal'd in the Union cause—
Prejudged of slavish cowardice,
While many a taunt and foul device
Came weekly forth with Harper's sheet,
To feed that base, infernal cheat.

But how they would themselves demean,
Has since most gloriously been seen.
'Twas seen at Milliken's dread bend!
Where e'en the Furies seemed to lend
To dark Secession all their aid,
To crush the Union Black Brigade.

The war waxed hot, and bullets flew
  Like San Francisco's summer sand,
But they were there to dare and do,
  E'en to the last, to save the land.
And when the leaders of their corps
  Grew wild with fear, and quit the field,
The dark remembrance of their scars
  Before them rose, they could not yield:
And, sounding o'er the battle din,
  They heard their standard-bearer cry—
"Rally! and prove that ye are men!
  Rally! and let us do or die!
For war, nor death, shall boast a shade
  To daunt the Union Black Brigade!"

And thus he played the hero's part,
  Till on the ramparts of the foe
A score of bullets pierced his heart,
  He sank within the trench below.
His comrades saw, and fired with rage,
Each sought his man, him to engage
In single combat. Ah! 'twas then
The Black Brigade proved they were men!
For ne'er did Swiss! or Russ! or knight!
  Against such fearful odds arrayed,
With more persistent valor fight,
  Than did the Union Black Brigade!

As five to one, so stood their foes,
When that defiant shout arose,
And 'long their closing columns ran,
Commanding each to choose his man!
And ere the sound had died away,
Full many a ranting rebel lay
Gasping piteously for breath—
Struggling with the pangs of death,

From bayonet thrust or shining blade,
Plunged to the hilt by the Black Brigade.
And thus they fought, and won a name—
None brighter on the scroll of Fame;
For out of one full corps of men,
But one remained unwounded, when
The dreadful fray had fully past—
All killed or wounded but the last!

And though they fell, as has been seen,
Each slept his lifeless foes between,
And marked the course and paved the way
To ushering in a better day.
Let Balaklava's cannons roar,
And Tennyson his hosts parade,
But ne'er was seen and never more
The equals of the Black Brigade!

Then nerve thy heart, gird on thy sword,
For dark Oppression's ruthless horde
And thy tried friends are in the field—
Say which shall triumph, which shall yield?
Shall they that heed not man nor God—
Vile monsters of the *gory rod*—
Dark forgers of the *rack* and *chain:*
Shall *they* prevail—and Thraldom's reign,
With all his dark unnumber'd ills,
Become eternal as the hills?
No! by the blood of freemen slain,
On hot-contested field and main,
And by the mingled sweat and tears,
Extorted through these many years
From Afric's patient sons of toil—
Weak victims of a braggart's spoil—
This bastard plant, the Upas tree,
Shall not supplant our liberty!

But in the right, our sword of power
We'll firmly grasp in this dread hour,
And in the life-tide's crimson flow
Of those that wrong us, write our No!
No! by all that's great and good;
No! by a common brotherhood,
The wrong no longer shall prevail,
Its myriad horrors to entail!

Better in youth pass off life's stage,
Battling 'gainst a tyrant's rage,
Than live to three-score years and ten,
Disown'd of God, despised of men;
Better that cities, hamlets, towns,
And every hut where life abounds,
In conflagration's ruins lie,
Than men as things should live and die;
Better the whetted knife be brought,
And quick as lightning speeds a thought,
Hurl life all wreaking from its throne,
Than live their manhood to disown,
Sooner than bear a hell of pain,
And wear a festering, galling chain,
To hoary age e'en from their birth,
And die the meanest thing on earth.

There is no deed they should not do,
Could they thereby obtain the clue,
The motive power and the might
To set their outraged people right!
Then grasp the sword, discard the sheath,
And strike for Liberty or Death!
But what is death? 'Tis, after all,
The merest transit from this ball
To some bright state or gloomy sphere,
Remote, perhaps—perhaps quite near.

And what is life? Hath it a charm,
While fetters gall the neck and arm,
And from no species of contempt,
However base, to be exempt?
'Tis true a noble bard hath said
That to the regions of the dead
"What dreams *may* come, *now* give us pause."
But who can so thwart Nature's laws
As to evade that dread unknown,
Through aid or effort of his own?

But is there aught to haunt a dream,
That man should so unwelcome deem,
As to regard it worse than stripes—
Worse than slavery's mildest types?
No, no! there's nothing, rest assured,
In life or death to be endured—
There are no tortures to excel
The fires of a Southern hell!
The lash, the yoke, the gag, the chain,
May each produce a world of pain;
But what are these, though all combined,
To gross sterility of mind?

To chain and scourge this mortal frame,
It were a sin and burning shame;
But who can estimate the doom
Of those that quench and shroud in gloom
The only lamp which God hath given,
To light the soul in earth or heaven?
While this external will expand,
In proud defiance of the brand,
The mind, that germ of tender growth—
That plant of far transcendent worth,
Will neither bud nor bloom nor bear,
Where thraldom's breath infects the air.

Then onward roll, thou dreadful War,
    If thou, and thou alone, canst bring
The boon of Freedom from afar;
    Roll darkly on then, while we sing:
We would not have thee slack thy speed,
    Nor change the tenor of thy way,
Till each infernal law and creed
    That fosters wrong, is swept away!
If needs be, lay proud cities waste!
    And slay thy thousands at a meal!
But in thy wake let Freedom haste,
    With oil to soothe and balm to heal.

————

AND here permit me to diverge
From real to fancy's flow'ry marge,
And sing of what I seem'd to see
While there, enshrined in reverie.
The past, and what is yet to be
Reveal'd in blank futurity,
Swept like a phantom through my brain,
Of which some shadows still remain:
And to those shadows let me call
The eye and silent ear of all.

One evening, wrapp'd in pensive mood,
    On fancy's wing I soar'd afar,
Till, seeing and unseen, I stood
    Amid the hidden springs of War:
And there, upon a canvas vast,
I saw this cruel war sweep past—
Its former battles fought again,
With all the unfought in their train.
Upon the sea and on the shore
Each battle scene, was marked with gore;

And bleaching there, on sea and plain,
Lay mangled bodies of the slain.
Of some were nothing save their trunk,
Whose life the thirsty earth had drunk:
With legs and arms all torn away
By some dread shell's destructive play;
And massive trees ball-riven stood,
All draped with powder, drenched with blood,
While clotted hair and flesh still clung
Their sear'd and shattered boughs among.
And 'neath the deep and angry waves,
Thousands had found their liquid graves:
And sleeping there 'mid shells and rocks,
Were many braves with fleecy locks.
Of such were many of the slain,
On every battle-field and plain.

But wild to pierce futurity,
Its deep veiled ultimatum see,
And learn the final of this war—
The waning of our evil star—
I turned the tardy canvas from,
And sped me on, when lo! a bomb,
Deeper in tone than aught I'd heard—
So deep the very earth was stirr'd,
As though the gods, in wrath or sport,
Had touch'd some pillar of their court;
Of Peace it was the harbinger—
The long-prayed, welcome messenger.

But eager still, I onward sped,
Unknowing why, or whither led,
Till in my path an angel rose,
My further progress to oppose.
His form was tall and passing fair—
His raiment like the driven snow,

And trod he on the ambient air
As mortals walk the earth below.
  His voice, though soft, seemed to expand,
And e'en in compass to increase,
  Till every nook of our fair land
Rang with the joyous song of PEACE!
Peace! and the loud-mouth'd cannon's roar
In silence slept, to wake no more!
Peace! and the soldier quits the field,
And doffs his corslet, sword and shield,
And in the burden of his lay,
The din of battle died away:
And lilies bloom'd and olives spread
In rich profusion o'er the dead.

  The dark Rebellion had been crushed,
And every wailing sound was hushed;
And there was not a slavish chain
In all Columbia's fair domain.
And then and there I saw unfold,
All fresh and bright from Freedom's mould,
A real Republic—such a one
As should have passed from sire to son;
A real Republic—free! uncurs'd!
The sole intention of the first—
In which the bright Damascus blade
Became the farmer's plowing spade:
And with the spear he pois'd of yore
His golden harvest did secure.

  And far away as the eye could span,
In its vast sweep from strand to strand,
I saw no South, North, East nor West,
But one broad land, all free and blest;
And there was not a jarring sound
In all the vastitude profound—

No wail, no sob, no sigh, no tear,
To dim the eye or mar the ear.
And violets bloomed the banks along,
And the lark poured forth his matin song,
And the lowly cot and massive dome
Had each the air of a joyous home;
And temples rear'd their spires on high,
Pointing away to the clear blue sky;
And myriad souls had gathered there,
Whose grateful hearts went up in prayer
To the God of love, whose gracious hand
Had clothed in peace their bleeding land.

———

WITH one allusion, we have done
The task so joyously begun:
It is to speak, in measured lays,
Of him the Nation loves to praise.

When that inspired instrument,
The subject of this great event,
Forth from the Halls of Congress came,
With even justice as its aim,
'Twas deem'd by some a fiendish rod,
But otherwise adjudged of God,
Who, turning earthward from His throne,
Beheld great Lincoln all alone,
With earth-bent brow, in pensive mood,
Pondering o'er some unsubdued
And knotty problem, half dissolved,
And half in mystery yet involved.

The interest of a continent,
All broken up by discontent—
His own dear land, land of his love,

The fairest 'neath the realms above—
Weighed down his form and rack'd his brain,
And filled his patriot heart with pain.
But when his mind conceived the thought
    To WRITE FOUR MILLION CAPTIVES FREE!
An angel to his conscience brought
    Approving smiles of Deity;
And ere he had with flesh conferr'd,
    He gave the bright conception birth,
And distant nations saw and heard,
    And bless'd his mission on the earth.

And we today reiterate,
With warmth of heart and depth of soul,
God bless Americ's Magistrate!
Long may he live to guide, control;
Long may that arching brow and high—
That spiritual and piercing eye:
That tall, majestic, manly form—
Live, our rainbow 'midst the storm;
And when the roar of battle's pass'd;
When vain Secession's breath'd his last;
When peace and order are restored,
And Freedom sits at every board;
And when the Nation shall convene
In mass, as ne'er before was seen,
And render eulogistic meeds
To worthy heroes' noble deeds,
A lengthened train shall claim their boast,
But LINCOLN's name shall lead the host!
His name shall grow a household word,
Where'er the human voice is heard;
And tribes and peoples yet unborn,
Shall hail and bless his natal morn.

AUGUSTUS ST. GAUDENS' CELEBRATED STATUE OF
ABRAHAM LINCOLN
LINCOLN PARK, CHICAGO, ILLINOIS

Abolition of Slavery in District of Columbia.

Thank God! from our old ensign
    Is erased one mark of shame,
  Which leaves one less to rapine,
    One less to blight our fame.
For two and sixty summers
  Has our broad escutcheon waved,
Amid the ceaseless murmurs
  And wails of the enslaved;
But in the blest hereafter
  Shall our oft afflicted ears,
Be solaced with bright laughter,
  With gladsome praise and cheers.
For freedom's altar's basis
  More permanent shall be,
When rid the gaunt embraces
  Of fell barbarity.

*   *   *   *   *   *   *

If Congress hath the power
  To expel from ten miles square
The Goliath of the hour,
  And charge the tainted air
With the pure breath of freedom,
  As to baffle all return,
Should they not e'en from Sodom,
  The vaunted monster, spurn?
Roaring like distant waters,
  Which no power can repress,
Up from ten thousand quarters
  Comes the responsive yes!
Yes! yes; our nation's banner
  We should purge from all its stains,
Nor yield to might nor manner,
  Till Right triumphant reigns.

THE PROGRESS OF LIBERTY.

Dedicated to Rt. Rev. Jabez Pitt Campbell, bishop of
the A. M. E. church, as a slight tribute to his many
noble qualities, his exalted piety, and his labors in
behalf of his oppressed race.

———

Introductory Note.

The "Progress of Liberty" is delineated in the
events of the past four years—the overthrow of the
rebellion, the crushing of the spirit of anarchy, the
total extinction of slavery, and the return of peace and
joy to our beloved country.

The invincibility of Liberty is illustrated in the
beautiful episode of the Swiss patriot, William Tell,
wherein the goddess is personified by an eagle tower-
ing amidst the clouds.

The poet claims the full enfranchisement of his race
from political, as well as personal thraldom, and declares
that the "Progress of Liberty" will not be complete
until the ballot is given to the loyal freedmen.

The noble actions and self-sacrificing spirit of the
immortal Lincoln is next sung, and in mournful strains
the poet bewails his martyrdom. This concludes with
a touching eulogy on our sainted martyr.

The reconstruction policy of President Johnson is
reviewed, and, while objecting, the poet does not wholly
condemn his motives, but warns the ruling powers that,
unless the spirit of rebellion is wholly obliterated and
every vestige swept away, it will only slumber to awake
again with renewed ferocity.

The Progress of Liberty.

ever, in all the march of time,
    Dawned on this land a more sublime
    And grand event, than that for which
    Today the lowly and the rich,
    From thrice ten thousand altars, send
Their orisons to God, their friend.

The severance of the bondsman's chain;
    The opening wide the prison door,
And ushering in this glorious reign
    Of liberty, from shore to shore,
Has formed an epoch in the life
    Of this great nation, that shall stand
And consecrate to sanguine strife,
    The full redemption of the land.

Hail! hail! glad day! thy blest return
    We greet with speech and joyous lay.
High shall our altar-fires burn,
    And proudly beat our hearts today.
And thou, thou ancient holiday!
    We hail thee with a new delight,
Since hope's bright beams and freedom's ray
    Have dawned upon the bondsman's night—
Dawned on his night and interspersed
    A deathless yearning to be free;
A heaven-approved and burning thirst,
    That naught can quench but *liberty*.

O, Liberty, what charm so great!
    One radiant smile, one look of thine
Can change the drooping bondsman's fate,
    And light his brow with hope divine.
His manhood, wrapped in rayless gloom,
    At thy approach throws off its pall,
And rising up, as from the tomb,
    Stands forth defiant of the thrall.
No tyrant's power can crush the soul
    Illumed by thine inspiring ray;
The fiendishness of base control
    Flies thy approach as night from day.

Ride onward, in thy chariot ride,
    Thou peerless queen; ride on, ride on—
With Truth and Justice by thy side—
    From pole to pole, from sun to sun!
Nor linger in our *bleeding South,*
    Nor domicile with race or clan;
But in thy glorious goings forth,
    Be thy benignant object Man.

Of every *clime,* of every *hue,*
    Of every *tongue,* of every *race,*
'Neath heaven's broad, etheral blue;
    Oh! let thy radiant smiles embrace:
Till neither slave nor one oppressed
    Remain throughout creation's span,
By thee unpitied and unblest
    Of all the progeny of *man.*

We fain would have the world aspire
To that proud height of free desire,
That flamed the heart of Switzer's Tell
(Whose archery skill none could excel),
When once upon his Alpine brow,

He stood reclining on his bow,
And saw, careering in his might—
In all his majesty of flight—
A lordly eagle float and swing
Upon his broad, untrammeled wing.

He bent his bow, he poised his dart,
With full intent to pierce the heart;
But as the proud bird nearer drew,
His stalwart arm unsteady grew,
His arrow lingered in the groove—
The cord unwilling seemed to move,
For there he saw personified
That freedom which had been his pride;
And as the eagle onward sped,
O'er lofty hill and towering tree,
He dropped his bow, he bowed his head;
He could not shoot—'twas Liberty!

For men have ever been disposed
    To crush their weaker fellows down;
Their selfish natures stand opposed
    To the heart's free, aspiring bound.
For e'er, since Time his march began,
Or mighty rivers seaward ran,
In greater or in less degree
The world's been cursed by slavery.

Nor has the system been confined
To any nation, race or kind;
The *Celt,* the *Saxon* and the *Dane,*
Each, in their turn, have worn the chain;
Each have been slaves—each bought and sold;
Their blood-price paid in paltry gold,
And from their kinships, loved and lorn,
To distant lands by strangers borne,

Where suffered they full many a wrong—
And where in bondage served they long.
Though long enthralled, yet there remains
Not e'en a vestige of their chains;
And were it not for history's lore,
The buried fact none could explore.
Freedom has swept their chains away
And clothed them with a brighter day.
For in despite all efforts made,
There e'er has been a certain grade
In the enslavement of a race,
At which reaction takes its place;
A point at which the crushed to earth,
Impelled by irate manly worth,
Throw off the yoke, discard the brand,
And claim their peerage in the land!
They rise, and fate proclaims the hour;
They seize the reigns and march to power.

As in the past, so shall it be
    Through all the unborn years afar;
Till earth is wholly purged and free,
    Will man 'gainst man go forth to war.
Wake, in your minds the sleeping world,
    From Eden's banished pair till now,
Behold war's crimson flag unfurled
    On every plain and mountain brow.
The sword has been the pioneer—
    The civilizer of mankind—
The John the Baptist sent to clear
    The way and fix the erring mind;

And the priest, with Bible spread,
Walks more securely where the tread
Of the swordsman in his wrath
Has left his foot-prints in the path.

Nor could the sciences unfold
Their wings that's purer far than gold,
Had not the savage in the breast
Of savage men been put to rest.

Thus, on her even-tenored way
    Fair truth has ever kept her course,
Battling now with fell delay—
    Now sweeping on with matchless force.
In mystic armor, bright and fair,
    Her braves stand mailed 'gainst dread despair.
Hence, they who battle for the right
    Are always stronger than the foe,
And only need the radiant light
    Of liberty their strength to know.
Although its light may be withdrawn,
    And error's blackening clouds increase,
Yet time will bring the glorious dawn
    Of Liberty and Truth and Peace.
Their strength, numerically viewed,
    May seem but nothing in the scale;
Yet, if their hearts are each imbued
    With liberty, they cannot fail;
For they who fight for liberty,
    They fight to conquest or to death,
And gain their proudest victory
    When the cause receives her breath.

Though error's numerous hosts array
    The march of freedom to impede,
'Twere vain: no forces can delay
    A Heaven-commissioned mortal need.
The wrong cannot forever last—
    The right is mightier than the chain,
And in the future, as in the past,
    Liberty must and shall obtain.

The tyrant's hand may firmly clasp
And strive to hold within his grasp
Those whom his baseness has betrayed—
His fiendish nature helped degrade—
Yet, in power and might and main,
Liberty must and shall obtain.

The bondsman's gloomy night has passed;
    The slavery of this land is dead;
No tyrant's power, however vast,
    Can wake it from its gory bed.
For in the order of events,
    And after an ignoble reign,
It died.   None mourned its going hence,
    Nor followed in its funeral train;
Ignoble birth, ignoble life,
    Ignoble death, ignoble doom!
Conceived by fiends in deadly strife,
    And cast into a nameless tomb.

Though slavery's dead, yet there remains
A work for those from whom the chains
Today are falling one by one;
Nor should they deem their labor done,
Nor shrink the task, however hard,
While it insures a great reward,
And bids them on its might depend
For perfect freedom in the end.

Commend yourselves through self-respect;
    Let self-respect become your guide:
Then will consistency reflect
    Your rightful claims to manhood's pride.
But while you cringe and basely cower,
    And while you ostracise your class,
Heaven will ne'er assume the power
    To elevate you as a mass.

In this yourselves must take the lead;
    You must yourselves first elevate;
Till then the world will ne'er concede
    Your claims to manhood's high estate.
Respect yourself; this forms the base
    Of manhood's claim to man's regard.
Next to yourself, respect your race,
    Whose care should be your constant ward;
Remember that you are a class
    Distinct and separate in this land,
And all the wealth you may amass,
    Or skill, or learning, won't command
That high respect you vainly seek,
    Until you practice what you claim—
Until the acts and words you speak
    Shall, in the concrete, be the same.

Screen not behind a pallid brow;
    Paint lends no virtue to the face;
Until the Black's respected, thou,
    With all the branches of his race,
Must bow beneath the cruel ban
    And often feel the wrinkled brow
Bent on you by a fellow-man
    Not half so worthy, oft, as thou.

Away with caste, and let us fight
    As men, the battles of the free,
And Heaven will arm you with the might
    And power of man's divinity.
There may be causes for distrust,
And many an act that seems unjust;
But who, when taking all in all,
    And summing up our present state,
Would find no objects to extol,
    No worthy deeds to emulate?

If such there be, deem him confessed
  Before the shrine of liberty
As one that would the truth arrest
  And crush to earth humanity;
For who, unless their sympathies
  Are with the spoilers of the poor,
Could heedless pass realities
  So fraught with freedom's genial lore?
Although the car of freedom moves
  Less swift by far than we desire,
Yet stations gained and passed should prove
  The destined goal is drawing nigher.

What though upon some distant verge,
  Or in some rayless cave or den,
The cruel, fiendish tyrant's scourge
  Doth still afflict the poor of men:
Has not the conquering arm of Right
  Become the power behind the throne?
Shall not the fell oppressor, Might,
  For all his ruthless acts atone?
To solve this query, ask not Tyre,
  Nor wander back to Greece or Rome;
But of the living now enquire,
  And read those foot-prints 'round your home.

Read but the record that appears
Upon the scroll of four short years,
And truth enough, I vow, you'll find
To satisfy an honest mind.

Four years ago fell slavery's reign
  Within this land was absolute;
The brand, the fetter and the chain
  Were forged for man as for the brute.

And in those ten miles square of earth,
    Which ever sacred should have been
To liberty and manly worth,
    The statesman sold and bought his kin;
For there the auction-block was seen,
    And hard by stood the whipping-post,
Where oft, alas! from fiendish spleen,
    The poor have yielded up the ghost.

Four years have gone, and now that square
    Of two-score miles in circuit round,
Freights every passing breath of air
    With freedom's grand and joyous sound.
The whipping-post, the slaver's mart,
    The scourge, the brand, the yoke, the chain,
Have all been banished from the heart
    Of fair America's domain.

Four years ago, and there was not
    A sable freeman in this land;
Though thousands gloried in their lot,
    Yet were they all beneath the brand.
That foul rendition law, which gave
    To avarice unquestioned right
To seize the man deemed as a slave,
    And drag him down to thraldom's night,
Exposed six hundred thousand souls
    To insult, outrage and abuse,
In view of all the perjured scrolls
    That fiends incarnate could adduce;
But that base law and baser hearts
    Of those who gave it prominence,
Have each on earth performed their parts,
    And gone to their dread recompense.

Nor is this all that has been done
  In four short years beneath the sun:
Liberia has been recognized—
  Also the Haytian's island home;
And lo! a Negro undisguised
  Has preached within the Nation's dome!
And proud Columbia's highest court
  Receives a counselor elect,
Which gives the lie to the report
  That fain would rob us of respect,
While Taney, with curses on his grave,
  Has gone to stand that Judge before,
At whose dread bar the poorest slave
  Is judged a man, and he—no more.

Like Cana's wine, the last and best,
And far transcending all the rest,
Is that grand act for which we meet
Each New Year day to laud and greet—
The issuance of that blest decree
Through which the millions now are free.
We laud the act and laud the worth
Of the noble heart which gave it birth;
For which today we gladly raise
Our hands and hearts in grateful praise
To Him who spake, and lo! 'twas done;
Whose work is finished—e'er begun;
And while innumerous songs shall rise
In grand memorials to the skies,
The burden of all our songs shall be
To Lincoln, God and Liberty!
Sing, oh! my harp, one song of cheer
To that fond name we all revere;
Sing of his trust, sing of his love,
O, sing of his home in the realms above!
High on the towering spire of fame,

In bold relief stands out a name
Which time can ne'er efface or dim:
It is the peerless name of him
Who dared his frowning land despite,
Do what his conscience deemed as right;
Who dared proclaim, that all might hear,
The dawn of freedom's jubilant year.
And when the glorious news went forth,
It fell, like Heaven's benignant dew,
Upon the bondsmen of the south,
And all that wore the sable hue—
Not only those of sable hue,
But every lover of the right
Grasped his unsheathed sword anew,
And nerved his heart with tenfold might,
Determined to wipe out the stain —
The vile excresence to remove—
And free from each obnoxious ban
The home and country of his love.

Yon proclamation of the free
　Is now the living testament
Of that great soul of liberty,
　Whose heart conceived its continent,
Whose mission was to rend the chain
　And let the long oppressed go free;
And having wholly filled his reign,
　He laid aside mortality
And donned the vesture of the spheres,
　And passed beyond our mortal ken,
To regions far remote from men—
　Where all that's great and good appear.
Though gone from earth, he is not dead;
　The great, the good, they never die;
But when these transient forms they shed,
　In fadeless youth they bloom on high.

Oh! could we pass beyond the doom
  And range through fields forever fair,
Arrayed in Heaven's eternal bloom,
  We'd find our benefactor there.

The Moses kind Heaven in mercy had lent
To lead us away from our discontent,
For we, like Israel, were oppressed,
And long our bleeding hearts' unrest
Has fallen on the dewy night,
While pleading with the Infinite.
The orbit-lamps, which burn on high
And flood with joy the azure sky—
The silver moon and clouds that sweep
Athrough the far-off realms so deep,
Are all familiar with our woe,
And of our griefs how much they know:
For when from pleasure's jovial round
The careless world lay slumber-bound,
We've knelt and looked up through our tears,
And asked of Heaven, how many years
Shall vile injustice basely reign?
How many years from 'neath the chain
Shall Godlike man, a creature made
But one step lower in the grade
Of wisdom's all-creative skill
Than those bright heralds of His will
Which stand His throne forever by,
Or on their spotless pinions fly;
Pour forth upon the midnight air
The doleful wail of his despair;
And oft from out the lunar heaven
Glad signs of promise have been given.
A Moses has been typified—
A prophet and a people's guide;

And we by faith have looked away
Beyond the night to the glorious day,
When in His strength the arm of God
Should rend the chain and break the rod,
And lead the oppressed from 'neath the brand
To manhood's joy in freedom's land.

Although intense the darkness grew,
As nearer still and nearer drew
The rising dawn ordained to bring
The day of promise on its wing,
And every hand against us turned,
And on us every passer spurned,
Yet, was our deathless trust the same
In Him who gave the sun his flame,
And spake from dark chaotic gloom
Bright worlds on worlds to live and bloom,
And by some deep, unfathomed source
Bound them forever to their course,
And on their broad and convexed face
To all the breathing tribes gave place;

To these that ply their finny oar,
And live where ocean thunders roar;
To those that float upon the breeze
And build their homes 'mid rocks and trees;
To those that prowl in quest of prey,
When night has closed the eye of day,
And those that serve and blessings bring,
With every beast and creeping thing,
And holds forever in His hands
The destiny of men and lands—
The destiny of every sphere
In heaven's blue fields remote or near,
While every creature He has made
Commands His care and special aid.

A God like this, we'd fain adore;
His friendship ours, our cause is sure.
As Israel, when they neared that sea
Whose waves rolled back with majesty,
And stood congealed in all their pride,
A liquid wall on either side;
Assembled on the farther strand,
And holding up their leader's hand,
They prayed, harped, danced and sung,
The aged mingling with the young,
While this refrain was heard afar,
"The Lord, the Lord's a Man of war,
And like no other God is He;
God of the whirlwind and the sea!"

And while they danced did Miriam sing:
"The Lord's my strength, the Lord's my king!"
Like them, we've halted on the shore,
To sing and tell our triumphs o'er.

The bondsman's chains at length are riven,
    The fettered limbs forever free;
Shout thou, O Earth, and thou, O Heaven,
    Proclaim the gladsome jubilee!

———

Now, to that feature of our lay
Involving interests of today—
Involving interests of the state—
Interests small and interests great;
The interest of the rich and poor—
Their interest now and evermore.

The rebels—crushed in their endeavor
To rend in twain this glorious land—
Are still its foes, and will forever
Upon the side of treason stand,
Till all the streets which lead to power
Freedom shall firmly barricade;
They'll wait in hope and pray the hour
Auspicious to their fiendish raid.

The panther changeth not his nature,
Though chained, is still a treacherous beast,
Seeking ever for his capture
And on his captor's life to feast.
To this extent doth bloody treason
Pervade the powerless rebel's heart;
They still are traitors, and bide their season
To hurl at truth their poisoned dart.

Look to those streets which lead to office:
'Tis long those by-paths they would come;
Place there a strong and trusty police;
Guard well the nation's classic dome.
Raise no seceder to position,
Place no foul traitor in command,
And thereby hinder a sedition
Deep as the base-work of our land.

Oh, let it not in truth be spoken,
For four long years we've war'd in vain;
The gordian knot remains unbroken,
And we are yet beneath the chain,
And they, the plotters of secession,
Have still their rods above our head,
Extorting from us a concession
E'en in the face of all our dead.

Where is that fiend-like will which fostered
    The dark rebellion at the first?
Deem it not dead, or e'en exhausted—
    It waits its time to slake its thirst,
And in an hour the least expected,
    And from a source we little deem—
When liberty's the least protected,
    'Twill start again the crimson stream.

Unless the roots are all extracted,
    The cancer will return again;
For partial surgery, when enacted,
    Imperils life, engenders pain.
Unless the causes which incited
    This fearful war we now remove,
The torch again will be ignited—
    And peace an airy bubble prove.

Of what avail is their parolment—
    What vow so sacred could they make,
That, once released from war's controlment,
    Their perjured natures would not break?
There are no oaths, nor vows can alter
    The life-long purpose of the heart;
Though firmly pledged, man will not falter
    When chance proclaims to play his part.

Go, ferret out those vile seceders—
    Seek them anear, seek them afar,
And bring to justice all their leaders—
    Base plotters in this bloody war.
Be they bishops, priests or laymen,
    Bring them, nor through pity spare;
Confine them where the truth placed Haman—
    Confine them in the middle air.

There let them swing from early morning
   Till night shall wrap the earth in gloom,
A fit rebuke and needful warning
   To all who chance escape their doom;
That ne'er again while Sol illumines
   The regions of unbounded space,
May dark, mysterious, fearful omens
   O'erspread our land with such disgrace.

Oh, ye, who claim to scan the future,
   And read for man—unborn events,
Pray tell us what shall be the nature
   Of the bondsmen's future tense;
Shall they, from whom the yoke has fallen,
   From whom the fetter has been loosed,
Aspire to no loftier calling,
   But still live on to be abused?

And will this land of boasted freedom,
   In whose defense our braves have died,
Now, when the cause no more doth need them,
   Remand them back without a guide,
And institute no laws to shield them
   From the brutal acts of those,
Who long in abject bondage held them,
   Whose heart no love nor pity knows?

Those swarthy troops, who bore their rifles,
   And bravely fought the nation's foe,
Regarding e'en their lives as trifles
   Compared with freedom's overthrow,
Won them laurels, and should inherit
   The ballot as their rightful due;
Aye, should inherit, if deeds of merit
   E'er merit aught that's good and true.

'Tis not enough, to rend the fetter;
   'Tis not enough, to part the chain—
The soldier merits something better—
   A full erasure of his stain,
That future years, in their enfolding,
   May of those wrongs no vestige find—
No shadowy clue to base withholding
   Of human rights from human kind.

There is no civil right that can equal
   The ballot in a freeman's hand;
It is the apex and the sequel
   To all that's noble, great and grand.
The poorest of the land invested
   With the *ballot,* may stand erect,
And pass this life through unmolested,
   Commanding ever a respect.

Rescind all systems of oppression;
   Raise all men to a common plain;
And there will not of vain secession
   Nor root, nor limb, nor branch remain.
O! give Columbia's swarthy subjects—
   The valiant-hearted and the true—
A noble base for future prospects;
   Give them the ballot—as their due.

Their due for deeds of manly bearing,
   Whene'er the chances were revealed,
And for their brave, chivalric daring
   On many a hot-contested field.
Give it for victories won the nation,
   And often, too, 'gainst fearful odds,
Such as, at times, to keep their station,
   Appeared a mystery to the gods.

Now, in your memories backward wander,
  And near Fort Hudson take your stand;
Where you may in safety ponder
  Upon the fearful and the grand.

———

Hark! hark! that deafening sound pervading
  The hills anear and hills afar;
Lo! 'tis the charge and cannonading
  Of the veteran hosts of war.
Look you kindly on that battle—
  The former slaves are in that fight!
They, who have herded long with cattle,
  Are warring for the freeman's right.

From off the earthworks of the foemen,
  See how the grape and bullets fly—
Mowing down my hardy yoemen,
  As doth the scythe the autumn rye;
But onward! onward! nothing daunted,
  Sword unsheathed or hand on spring,
To where those murderous guns are planted,
  Whose mighty force those missiles fling.

Now, see them, as the foe advances,
  With sabres drawn, on hurried feet;
They halt, and now they poise their lances,
  And now the fierce combatants meet.
The former slave and former master—
  See how furiously they rave;
Which shall outlive the disaster,
  The master or his former slave?

List to their swords and sabres clashing,
    As slave confronts his tyrant lord;
See! see them, at each other dashing—
    Now, see them writhing on the sward!
See the struggling; hear the screaming;
    Hear the curse and hear the prayer;
See the crimson life-tide streaming
    From their sword-points through the air.

Now the blacks are beaten backward—
    Backward beaten by the foe;
And now again they rally onward;
    On to the breastwork, on they go!
The walls are gained, their braves have scaled
        them;
    Behold the stars and stripes on high!
The former masters' hearts have failed them;
    See! see! before their slaves they fly.
See on the field the dead, the wounded—
    Fallen, fallen to rise no more;
Beside them, see their sabres grounded,
    All reeking still with human gore.

And shall the heroes of such battles,
    Who fought for liberty for all,
Again be classed with goods and chattels—
    With beasts of burden in the stall?
Shall patriots have their rights contested,
    And thereby forced to wear a brand,
While heartless rebels are invested
    With all the honors of the land?
Ye men who prize Columbia's honor;
    Ye who should guide her in the right:
Oh, suffer not this base dishonor;
    Let naught so foul her glory blight.

Remove your doubts, dispel your fears,
  And in the right move bravely on;
For ere one round decade of years
  Have passed, full liberty shall dawn.
Your every right shall be obtained,
  And you respected here shall be;
Here in this land, where long enchained,
  You've worn the badge of slavery;
While here we sing of liberty
  Upon this far-off western strand,
The soul-inspiring symphony
  Is welling up o'er all the land.

For lo! Arkansas doth rejoice,
And Texas sings with cheerful voice,
And Mississippi's heart doth swell,
And hail with joy the rising knell
Now sounding on her gulf-bound coast—
The dirge of a departed ghost.
And Louisiana's fields of cane
Doth wave in triumph the refrain;
And Alabama's lofty pines,
And Florida's sweet-scented vines
Today doth joyously exhale
Rich odors on each passing gale.
And Georgia, freed from every vice,
Now offers up her fields of rice—
And South Carolina—first to err—
Repentant of the days that were,
Now waves her chainless hands on high,
In praise of freedom's victory.
And North Carolina's Dismal Swamp,
Arrayed in rich and gorgeous pomp,
Doth hail with pride the loud acclaim,
And sweetly sing in freedom's name.
And Old Virginia, proud and grand,

With her fair sister, Maryland,
Doth chant the chorus, swell the song,
The which today shall roll along
In pæans deep, and loud, and strong,
O'er every hill and vale and plain
Throughout the land, from Gulf to Maine,
And in one grand halo of sound,
Sweep fair Columbia's distant bound,
And on the radiant wings of light
Soar upwards to the Infinite,
And pour upon the Eternal's ear
One song and shout of grateful cheer.

And now, my muse, thy song resume,
   'Twixt hope and doubt, 'twixt joy and fear,
'Twixt morning gray and twilight gloom,
   Along a path nor dark, nor clear—
Sing now of him in high estate,
   On whom is bent the nation's eye—
Where all her glories culminate
   To form a radiance for her sky.
The now incumbent of that chair
   Where he, our good friend, sat before—
Has spoke full oft and loud and clear,
   Within the audience of the poor.

And poorer none than those that wait
   And feeless serve his native state—
A shoeless, coatless, hatless throng,
   Who ne'er have deemed the journey long,
If 'twere to catch his words and smiles,
Between them lay a score of miles;
With hasty feet they'd wend their way—
No child in heart more blessed than they,
With but one word, or e'en a look
From him who had his friends forsook,

And stood apledged before high Heaven,
That he would see their fetters riven:
That he would be their fathful guide,
And lead them past the crimson tide,
Athrough the wilderness that lay
Between their night and that bright day
Which shines forever on the rest
Of all the worthy, free and blest;

That he their Moses would become
And bring them to the freeman's home—
That he their cause would ne'er forsake,
Nor his pledge nor promise break,
Till every bondsman in the land
Should on the plains of freedom stand—
Pledged to the sacred cause of truth;
Pledged in the early days of youth;
Pledged by the summer, the winter and spring,
And pledged by all that truth may bring.

And now, that he sits in high estate
And holds the interests of the great;
The interest of the passing poor —
Their interest now and evermore
Within the hollow of his hand,
Oh! will he, will he firmly stand?
Or, in the mantlings of the just
Will he betray his sacred trust?

Forbid it, Heaven! O, Heaven, forbid!
And moisten not the trusting lid
With scalding teardrops from the heart,
Which needs must flow should he depart
Now, from the sacred cause of truth,
And from the pledges of his youth.
To these, oh, may he ever stand!

Firm as the mountains of his land!
And from his high, majestic place,
Look favoring on an injured race,
And use his Heaven-entrusted might,
To raise them from oppression's night,
And in this all-auspicious hour,
Invest them with a freeman's power:
Whereby they may themselves protect
Against the wiles of base neglect,
And cause this glorious land to be,
In fact, the home-land of the free.

Then shall mankind call him blest,
And when he sinks to his quiet rest,
From that bright, hoary autumn, he will look
        back and see
This broad land—all happy and free.

Modern Moses, or "My Policy" Man.

There is a tide in men's affairs,
Leading to fame not wholly theirs—
Leading to high positions, won
Through noble deeds by others done.
And crowns there are, and not a few,
And royal robes and sceptres, too,
That have, in every age and land,
Been at the option and command
Of men as much unfit to rule,
As apes and monkeys are for school.

For seldom an assassin's blow
Has laid a benefactor low
Of any nation, age or clime,
In all the lengthened march of time,
That has not raised to power and might,
Some braggart knave or brainless wight,
Whose acts unseemly and unwise,
Have caused the people to despise
And curse the hours of his reign,
And brand him with the marks of Cain.
And yet to crown the mystery,
All these have had a *Policy*.

Though Cain was treach'rous and unjust,
And smote a brother to the dust—
'Tis not of him we wish to speak,
Nor of the wife he went to seek;
Nor of the blood his Nimrod spilt,
Or famous city which he built.

But choose we rather to discant,
On one whose swaggish boast and rant,
And vulgar jest, and pot-house slang,
Has grown the pest of every gang
Of debauchees wherever found,
From Baffin's Bay to Puget Sound.
And yet he occupies a sphere
And fills a more exalted chair,
(With arrogant unworthiness,
To his disgrace, I must confess),
Than any officer of State,
Or king, or princely magistrate
Of royal blood or noble birth,
Throughout the kingdoms of the earth.

But how he chance attain'd that hight,
Amid the splendor and the light,
The effulgent glory and the ray
Of this the nineteenth century,
May, to the superficial mind,
Seem much complexed and undefined;
But when the dark and shameless truth,
Is properly ascribed to Booth,
The strangeness vanishes in haste,
And we through murder stand disgraced.
Disgraced! Perhaps some other word,
Or milder term should be preferred;
And if preferred, that term might be
Exposed to *My Policy.*

But there's a legend much in vogue,
The act of some *knave, wit* or *rogue,*
A sort of fabled heresy,
Clothed in the garb of prophecy;
In which 'tis said that "in the day,
When kith and kindred shall array,

Their hostile armies and engage
In deadly contest, youth and age,
Lo! from the people shall arise,
One of the people in disguise;
A man loquacious in his way,
And greatly given to display;
A self-wrought garment he shall wear,
And *beverage* be his constant fare;
Akin his normal state shall be,
To a ship unballas'd and at sea.

And he shall favor all that's mean,
Or low, or vicious and obscene;
And pay to neither age nor youth,
A due regard, nor e'en to truth—
And he shall by his subtle vows,
Induce the people to arouse,
And bear him in their confidence,
Toward a lofty eminence.
Just here occurs a short hiatus,
And then concludes the legend thus—
And he shall owe to tragedy,
His zenith of felicity;
And unto gross apostacy,
The basis of *My Policy.*"

But this is so obtuse, of course;
No one can really see its force;
And if they could, what is there in it
To claim attention for a minute—
Or, by which to point the hand,
To him the Chief of all the land?
In reason's name, in what relation
Could it refer to his high station,
Unless some bloody-handed fray,
Had to his office paved the way?

For you and I are well aware,
Just how he chanced obtain that chair;
For any *rustic lad* of skill,
Who knows the way to the nearest mill,
Would not regard the thing a task,
But say in substance, were he asked,
First and foully, through a stub and twist,
And then as the farmer claims his grist,
By being second on the list;
Why, 'tis just as plain to sanity,
As the logic of *My Policy*.

But as for *Mose,* he has been
And is to-day as free from sin
As that fond friend who kissed his Lord,
In presence of a Roman horde.
'Tis true he did somewhat disguise
His real intentions, and surprise
The loyal voters of the North,
By feigning hatred to the South;
Through which he gained their confidence,
And won that lofty eminence.

'Tis said, and yet I know not why,
His fingers wear a crimson dye,
The which retraced, would likely lead
Aback to some unlawful deed,
And only back perhaps, alas,
To constant pressure of the glass —
Or to his deep intensity,
Of interest in My Policy.

But, lest the treachery of the mind
Should chance forget a liege so kind,
We deem this quite a fitting place
To draw a picture of his grace.

His age, since men so far excel,
Their seemings none can rightly tell;
And some there are, on earth's broad stage,
Who do not really know their age;
Others who would not like their's told,
Lest some gay flame should deem them old.

But to the physiognomy
Of him, my liege, My Policy,
Of rather more than medium size,
A blooming nose and hazel eyes,
And mien, that one might think him given
To beverage, morning, noon and even';
And judge that his proboscis wore
Its crimson from the overstore;

For there are some rare nectars known
And taken to impart a tone
To the stomach, which will produce,
By repetition and abuse,
The like results; hence, many think
His glow the sad effects of drink;
Others, more prone to charity,
Ascribe it to *My Policy.*

'Tis said he wonders why it is,
That all the land makes such a phiz,
And why they keep in strict reserve,
A shield for the olfactory nerve;
When e'er My Policy is brought
Within the radius of their thought.

They surely do not see the point,
But act as though some out-of-joint
Machine had gained the track,
And now was keeping progress back.

O, is it not a burning shame,
That any folks with such a name
For science and philosophy,
To thus regard My Policy.

Sumner he claims is much at fault,
And Stevens plotting a revolt
Of Congress 'gainst the President,
And 'gainst his noble sentiment—
With which e'en Davis doth agree,
And all his learned constituency;
Hence, Sumner must not there remain,
And Stevens' might we ought restrain,
And Phillips should not be allowed
To exercise before the crowd,
His foul bombastic heresy,
In variance to *My Policy.*

His life he deems quite insecure,
And such a thought long to endure,
Is torturous in the extreme,
And breeds full many a fitful dream.
He fears some hireling knave may prove
Recreant to pretended love,
And give for *brandy,* water instead,
And thus consign him to the dead,
With all his virtue on his head.

His friends have counseled 'gainst alarm,
And 'gainst all apprehended harm,
And well they might, since few are more
From hurt and violence secure.
For those who practice lawless deed,
And on the life of virtue feed,
Are not accounted with his foes,
But now and e'er have been of those

Who would through nameless years protract
His office and his life intact—
The dauntless sons of chivalry,
Who glory in *My Policy.*

'Tis said, that in the days agone,
He pledged himself to the forlorn;
He pledged himself the bondsman's friend,
And one on whom they might depend
For counsel, succor or redress,
In all their hours of wretchedness,
And swore that he would be their guide,
And lead them past the crimson tide,
And through the wilderness that lay
Between their night and that blest day
That shines forever on the rest
Of all the worthy, free and blest;
That he their *Moses* would become,
And lead them to a freeman's home
And swore that he would ne'er forsake
Them, nor his pledge or promise break,
Till every bondsman in the land
Should on the plains of freedom stand.

Pledged to the sacred cause of truth;
Pledged in the early days of youth;
Pledged by the summer, winter, spring,
And pledged by all the truth may bring;
With all these pledges on his soul,
And clothed with power to control
The future destiny of those,
His wards by all his recent oaths.

Mark well his action when for aid
Their suppliant prayer to him was made?
Witness an instance of his love,
And all your former doubts remove.

Mark when that bill for the supply
Of starving millions met his eye;
A breadless, clotheless, houseless throng,
Thus rendered by his nation's wrong.
Does he the bill in haste receive
And sign, their suff'rings to relieve?

Yes, if withholding of the cup
From parched lips, whereof one sup
Would quite allay an inward pain,
And quite restore to health again
A prostrate mortal, doomed to die,
Unless his needs met swift supply,
Can be accounted as relief—
Then he in their deep hour of grief,
Did them relieve and kept his vow;
When with a dark and wrinkled brow,
He stamped his veto on their prayer,
And doomed the suppliants to despair.

O, what a "Moses" he has been!
How strenuously against the sin
Of his fathers he has fought;
And how ingeniously besought
The nation in this trying hour,
To invest with all their wonted power
Our late rebellious, loving foes,
To whom for all our recent woes,
Our wasted treasure, wasted lives,
Our orphaned children, widowed wives,
Our prostrate cities, deserted farms,
And all the joys of wars alarms,
We are most deeply debtors all,
And in meek gratitude should fall
Prostrate before them in the dust,
And yield the nation to their trust:

And to enforce the reason why,
That we should not this boon deny,
Propounds with matchless dignity,
His ineffable—*My Policy.*

School'd in his childhood to regard
Foul treason worthiest of reward,
And loyalty an empty name,
Meriting dark reproach and shame;
Therefore, he deems the rebels more
Worthy positions than before;
Before their nameless deeds of horror
Spread o'er our land the veil of sorrow;
And fain would from the very scurf,
E'en as from the rising surf
Of rebeldom, at once create
Grand officers of high estate,
And bring them to the nation's court,
His grave *My Policy* to support.

'Tis said the clergy everywhere,
Have held up holy hands in prayer
For his redemption from the thrall,
And pit of his apostate fall;
But recently by dream or word,
Have been most signally assured,
That there are no blest agencies
Of grace, outside the promises,
And in that almost boundless plan,
Salvation offered unto man,
Are no provisions that embrace
A proffered pardon in his case;
That it were madness to bewail,
Since all their efforts can but fail;
For he, to use a term uncivil,
Has long been mortgaged to the Devil;

But the fact which no one knows,
Is why the deuce he don't foreclose.
Perhaps he entertains a doubt,
And fears that Mose might turn him out;
Hence, *His Satanic* Majesty's
Endorsement of *My Policy.*

He claims that suffrage, if applied
To Negroes, should be qualified;
That they diplomacied, should hail
From Dartmouth, Harvard or from Yale,
Before entrusted for an hour
With manhood's great elective power.

But every rebel in the land,
From Maine to Georgia's distant strand;
Though dark their minds as rayless night,
Should exercise this manly right,
Though destitute of reason's force
As Balaam's ancient riding horse:
On these the boon he would confer,
Without a scruple or demur,
Because these *gentlemen, quoth he,*
Are members of My Policy.

His vetoes—gracious! what a list!
Never in time did there exist
Such an array of negative,
Bombastic and explanative;
'Tis said their reasons are profound,
Their logic almost passing sound;
And that such lucid rays they shed,
They're understood before they're read.

The Bureau Bill is deemed the first
Of numerous acts, by him reversed;
The power that bill sought to confer
On him, provoked his just demur,
And for this strange, unlikely fault,
His meekness rose in fierce revolt,
And flamed with wrath and power to kill,
He hurled his veto at the bill;
For actions of humanity,
Accord not with *My Policy.*

He next reversed the bill of rights,
Lest all the girls—that is the whites—
Should Desdemonia's become,
And fly each one her cherished home,
And take to heart some sooty moor,
As Fathers did in days before.
If but the legal right were given,
He fears that six in every seven
Of all the maids in all the land,
Would give the matrimonial hand
Unto some swarthy son or other,
And some, perhaps, might wed a *brother.*

This horrid thought his wrath excites,
And swearing 'gainst all "woman's rights,"
He grasped the veto in his ire,
And doomed the *bill* to endless fire;
For all such reciprocity,
Was foreign to *My Policy.*
This ghost-like thought preyed on his soul,
And robbed him of all self control,
Till from his fears, lest they obtain,
He got the veto on the brain;
The inflated type, the very worst,
With which a mortal e'er was cursed.

And hence, when e'er an act is brought,
For which his signature is sought,
How plain soever the device,
He fancies that he "smells a mice,"
And forthwith runs the trap to bring
My Policy, and sets the spring,
And waits with pain-suspended cough,
To see the curious thing go off.

And when the fancied mouse is caught
Within his fancied trap of thought,
To hear him in that frenzied laugh,
And see that full three-fingered quaff
Pass down the lining of his throat,
And find a lodgment 'neath his coat,
Would crimson o'er the cheek with shame,
And send a tremor through the frame,
The which would cause the heart to yield
To poignant truth so oft revealed,
And in that act confess they see
The secrets of *My Policy*.

The little giant of the West—
His labor done, was laid to rest,
And to eternalize his fame,
And thus immortalize his name,
Moses, with vassals of renown,
Comes swinging past from town to town;
And makes a quite imposing tour,
Save that he proves himself a boor
At divers times in divers ways,
All through his eagerness for praise,
For e'en despite the peerless Grant,
And monument he came to plant,
All those that were not wholly blind,
Could see he had an axe to grind;

The monument was but a ruse,
A subtle means to introduce
My liege of graceless dignity,
The author of *My Policy.*
'Tis said that he at times would come
To cities which were not "to home;"
From which long ere the pageant closed.
The peerless Grant grew indisposed,
And to the banks of Erie's Lake,
Repaired for reputation's sake.

But be this statement false or true,
It has the smallest part to do
With the matter of fact at hand,
Which is this, when through the land
He'd gone and played the *knave and clown,*
In every city, village, town,
And felt *My Policy* was sure
To win by virtue of the tour,
The people rise in mass and vote,
And thus most signally denote
By their vote and by their voice,
And by the subjects of their choice,
That they had blindly failed to see
The beauties of *My Policy.*

Hence, when the massive cavalcade
Swung round and round in grand parade,
With much chagrin, they're all dispensed,
Just where their fruitless tour commenced.
'Tis said that Moses had a dream,
The which has been his constant theme
Of thought, and converse ever since,
It seems as though he can't convince
Himself that there in truth is not
Some pre-arranged, mischievous plot

In embryo, a thing accursed ;
And yet, ere long destined to burst
On him and from his famed renown
And apec glory, drag him down ;
Though but a dream, 'twas so akin
Unto a fact that should have been,
And because he does not know
But what it really may be so,
And like the general that was "lame,"
Who started ere the foeman came,
Has suddenly become distres't
With pains and achings in the breast—
'Tis said when *night* had laid him down
(His *sainted* form) in sleep profound,
There stole athwart his fevered brain
A dream which caused his spirit pain ;

It seemed that 'reft of every doubt,
His myriad sins had found him out,
And charged with numerous crimes and blood,
Before the bar he trembling stood,
And heard he all the evidence,
The prosecution and defense,
And heard the verdict of the court,
And felt the truth of their report ;
But that which seemed to pain him most,
And deepest heartfelt anguish cost,
Was not to find the charge sustained,
But 'twas to find himself constrained
Forthwith to abdicate and be
A martyr to *My Policy.*

The mansion rose in all its pride,
With all its sweetness multiplied
Its grand exterior, spotless white,
A nation's glory and delight—

Its massive portals swinging round,
Without a jar or grating sound—
Its Brussels carpet, velvet chairs,
Downy couches, levees and fairs,
O, from such rare joys to part,
It seemed as though 'twould break his heart.

What next occasioned much regret,
Was the receptions which he met;
For while he knew full many there,
Not one but with a scornful air,
Spurned on him as they passed him by,
As though they feared in coming nigh
Contamination might ensue,
And they grow leprosied and untrue;
Such ingrate acts were rather more
Than he could bear his cup ran o'er,
And streaming down his blooming face,
He felt the hot tears of disgrace;

He thought of Willy, and ran in haste,
But found that he had been displaced;
He next sought *Revey, Vall* and *Wood,*
But found them in a sullen mood,
Red-eyed and swollen, as though the three
Had been in perfect sympathy;
Before them sat a demijohn,
Partly filled and partly gone—
'Twas quite enough; he'd found the place,
He held the huge thing to his face,
Till through his hands it slipped and broke,
And springing forward, he awoke
And found himself stretched on the floor,
And loudly rapping at the door
Were wardens, whom from sleep profound,
Had been affrighted by the sound;

And to each other wildly calling,
To learn what ponderous thing had fallen.
"Go way," from the within was said,
"No one is hurt—*confound that bed;*"
Then gathering up his graceless form,
Exhausted some, and somewhat worn,
And opening wide his hazel eyes,
And gazing round in glad surprise,
Poured on the night's tranquility,
This strange and marked soliloquy—

"Can these bright scenes belie their seeming?
What means all this—have I been dreaming?
Surely, this is the mansion still,
Despite their numerous threats of ill;
Despite him and his numerous wiles,
I'm still the heir of fortune's smiles,
Despite them and their myriad threats,
Their aimless, soulless epithets;
I am still the President
Of proud Columbia's vast extent."

And forthwith from his breast a flask
He drew, and stripped it of its mask,
All sparkling to its very fill,
A goodly half-pint, less a gill,
The which in oriental style,
Dispatched he at a single smile;
Then threw the needless flask aside,
And with a pompous look of pride,
And seeming consequential air,
He sank into an easy chair,
And gravely mused upon the past,
And mused on subjects far too vast,
Except for some learned debauchee,
Or adept in My Policy.

O, were I but a dramatist,
What stores of thought I would enlist,
What telling words I would indite,
And what a play my pen should write;
I'd hie me to the nation's dome;
Amid its splendors I would roam,
Discant on palace, hall and court,
And on the nation's grave support,
Until I placed upon the stage
The grandest burlesque of the age;

"Moses! *Moses!*" should be my theme;
Not He that through the crimson stream
Led out from Egypt Israel's host;
But "our Mose" of rant and boast,
Who from the nation's balcony,
Cajoled a drunken revelry,
In telling words of pothouse lore,
The which had ne'er been heard before,
Since Kidd, the terror of the wave,
Placed men's life-chart within the grave.

Oh, Demosthenes! in silence rest,
Henceforth "our Mose" shall be the test
Of all oratorical display,
And for a sample, by the way,
Witness his chaste and classic art,
In his description of sweetheart,
And Penny nibbling at his heels,
And then how graphic he reveals
His wond'rous buncombe, and his pluck,
In that grave story of the duck.
And when you have read, O think of the stage,
And the wonderful *star* of a wonderful age!

Preface.

The wonderful change that has taken place in the political character of the United States, in the last ten years, is well calculated to excite the poetic feelings of any man having a spark of poesy in him.

The march of events have been peculiarly romantic, outstripping all human expectations, and leaving even prophecy in the rear.

The present poem is given to the public with the hope of perpetuating, to some extent, the remembrance of the "good time," and of sending to the future some little knowledge of the trials, struggles, and triumph of Liberty in our land.

The author felt his incompetency to do justice to the task—it being an unexplored field—but he has opened the way, and leaves to others the duty of following, if they will.

This poem was written during hours snatched from other occupations. Still, we send it forth, confident that the theme of which it treats, and the earnest sincerity of the author, will win for it the public approbation. It is a statement of facts—not fiction—and, gentle reader, we ask you to follow it to the close, trusting it may nerve you anew for the right, and encourage you in the cause of humanity.

HON. JOHN D. RICHARDS.

DETROIT, MICHIGAN.

The Triumph of Liberty.

TO HIS EXCELLENCY

HENRY P. BALDWIN,

Governor of the State of Michigan,

As a slight testimonial to his generosity of heart and
nobleness of mind, the following poem
is most respectfully inscribed.

That truth, than fiction, is more strange,
  There's not the shadow of a doubt,
When we regard the wondrous change
  One short decade has brought about.
The leopard may have changed his spots,
  Or the Ethiop changed his skin,
And would far less excelled our thoughts,
  Than those great changes which have been.
For nought exists in earth or air
  Or ocean's depths of endless shade,
With which we justly can compare
  The changes of the last decade.

Had one deep-skilled in mystic lore,
  Some favored heir or providence,
Proclaimed abroad from door to door
  The last decade's unborn events,
The multitudes who may have heard
  His auguries, though chastely clad,
Would have pronounced them most absurd,
  And their prognostic author mad.
Or, had an angel of the sky
  Left for a time his watch and ward,
And from some towering mountain high
  Cried mightily, thus saith the Lord!

Columbia's sons, a million strong
   Shall panoply themselves for war,
And o'er their hills and vales ere long
   To battle rush from near and far!
The century bound and fettered slave
   Shall grasp the hilt of freedom's sword
And rush amid the struggling brave
   And write his liberties restored;
He shall have faith where others doubt
   And onward press to lead the van,
Till slavery's stain he washes out
   In treason's gore, and stands a man.

And ere one full decade has passed
   The land redeemed shall proudly see,
Of slavery's relics e'en the last
   Engulfed in freedom's boundless sea.

Would we have deemed the message true,
   Brought by the heavenly ward so near,
And gave to it that reverence due
   A message from the glory sphere?
We might have lent a patient ear
   And thus the message have received,
We might have felt a sense of fear,
   But never would our hearts believed:

It would have been impossible,
   So wedded were we to the wrong,
Our hearts had grown invulnerable
   To all appeals however strong.

No message sent from hell or heaven,
   Brought by the living or the dead,
Could e'er the mighty spell have riven
   By which dark wrong and we were wed.

Our natures had been schooled to look
    Adversely on each phrase of right,
Until our hearts could proudly brook
    The truth made bare in reason's light—

For error's potent chords had twined
    About our hearts from early age,
Till like the tillers of the mind
    Our guides were they in every stage—
We could not comprehend the thought,
    That freedom was of native mold,
Heaven inspired and heaven taught
    Which neither chains nor cells can hold:
Therefore we could not reconcile
    The seeming gross absurdity,
That *he,* the slave and long reviled,
    Nursed yet the germs of liberty.

If not how could he rise above
    His present status of disgrace,
Or what incentive could him move
    The all auspicious to embrace?
But changes of the recent past
    Have swept our theories away,
And crowned with wonders unsurpassed
    The radiant glories of to-day.

———

WITHIN the lapse of one decade
More history we have lived and made
Than during all the years before,
Since first our fathers sped them o'er
The deep blue ocean's heaving breast,
And came to this proud land, the West.

And we have grown in moral hight
When viewed by heaven's or freedom's light,
More in these years a thousand fold
Than during all the years of old.

One decade back and every eye
That scann'd us closely saw the lie,
And turned from our spread banner's face
To men in chains, and cried disgrace,
And, hissing, pointed with disdain
At Freedom forging slavery's chain.
One decade back and slavery's beck
Alike held State and Church in check,
How grave or trivial the affair
On no account would either dare
To move one hair-breadth in extent
Till clothed with his august consent—
When e'er he waved his Sceptered hand
The mighty millions of our land
Were filled with wonderment and awe
And eager to obey his law—
He stamped his foot, and Liberty
Trembled as doth the aspen tree,
When old Boreas from his cave,
Begirt with wrath comes forth to rave.

The court, to do him honor, made
Him a license to invade
The lowly cot and palace dome,
And sacred precincts of each home,
Where ever found upon our soil
In quest of his assumptive spoil.
And men who ranked in high estate
Would breathless on his bidding wait,
And all our proud official corps,
Like blood-hounds, ran from door to door,

And often forced their presence where
E'en decency would cry forbear;
And all for what? Why, simply
This, and nothing more—Liberty!
Innate and deathless as the soul
Had swelled beyond the chains control,
And e'en inspired the base born slave
To seek for freedom or the grave.

Our prisons, too, whose chief intent
Was crime to punish and prevent,
Became the slave-pens of the land,
To which the Tyrant of the brand
To check-mate human liberty
Held in his grasp both lock and key.

Besides all this, a hoary sage,
  A highly honored legal chief
Just passing from this earthly stage,
  Gave this as his profound belief:

"Blacks have no rights, not life except,
Which bind the white man to respect."

This formed the climax of support
Which slavery drew from Freedom's Court.
While thus the *Court* strained every nerve
Her wonted fealty to preserve,
The *Church* was not a whit behind;
For she, with all her strength combined,
Was moving earth and fiends and hell
In order that she might excel
The baseness of the *Court,* and rise
Pre-eminent in *Slavery's* eyes.
To do him honor prelates came
Of nearly every creed and name,

All decked in sacerdotal gear,
Each rivaling each as to appear,
While void of ostentatious pride,
Most potent, grave and dignified.

And each to Court his reverence bowed,
And prayed to him both long and loud;
And temples reared they in his name,
And grand memorials to his fame,
Whose every brick and massive stone
Was purchased with a human bone,
And all the mortar 'twixt their layers
Was mingled flesh and blood and tears
Of captives, whom dark wrong had slain
To rear up Slavery's Godless fain.
And thus with rant hypocrisy
And sacrilegious blasphemy,
The Church sought to surpass the Court
In crowning slavery with support
Oh, if the cheek was ever flushed,
Of devils, then they must have blushed
At these base scenes of mammon greed,
Which hell itself could scarce exceed!
For there, midst all this mock display,
This scowl upon the face of day,
The truth lay prostrate, and the right
Was chained and gagged, while reason's light
Shone like a taper in a tomb,
And half extinguished by the gloom.
Oh! ne'er did goodly land thus sink
As ours so near to ruin's brink.

Our fathers might have wept, and did,
If earthly scenes are not all hid
From eyes of those blest ones who stand
Or near or far in glory land.

But unto God that's ever near,
The righteous are His special care;
And in our land there were a few
Firm friends of Freedom, tried and true.
A few who ne'er had bowed the knee
Nor sacrificed to Slavery;

A faithful, zealous noble band,
The salt and savors of our land,
Whose meritorious deeds should blaze
In letters of undying praise.
But while we thus them all revere,
Of two we'd fain make mention here.

ONE decade back there lived a man,
A strict, unswerving Puritan;
And though as brave as Ammon's son,
No gods had he to serve but one,
The God of Justice, God of Truth,
Whom he had served from early youth.

His heart was not inured to wrong,
Though he had seen and felt it long;
Yet had he oft implored the time
When there should be an end to crime,
When Truth should rise, assert her claim,
And wrong sink down to whence it came.

At length he grew to feel inspired
To what his heart had long desired,
To strike one blow for Liberty,
Where it should end in victory;
Though he should perish in the deed,
He felt that he could plant the seed
From which the harvest would arise,
And shrank not from the sacrifice;

Him call enthusiast, if you will,
Fanatic, or something wilder still,
It will not blur his deathless name,
Nor bar his onward march to fame.

For when he felt the hour had come
He left his fair North Elba home
And with e'en less than a score of men,
Went forth, and in the very den
And citadel of Slavery
Unsheathed his sword for Liberty.

This, this was old John Brown, the brave
Whom great Virginia hanged, to save
Through sacrifice to Slavery,
Her panic stricken chivalry.
For from the night on which he made
Their State the center of his raid,
Until the law pronounced him dead,
Of him they lived in constant dread.

Although confined within a cell,
By many a bolt and lock as well,
And prostrate on a fevered cot,
Through consequences ill-begot,
From care and pain and loss of blood,
And from the much he had withstood,
Besides all this, of armed men,
To guard that ancient veteran,
A regiment were scattered round,
All o'er that half enchanted ground,
Lest he should from his mat of straw,
Come forth and by his presence awe,
And terrify e'en unto death
Famed Chivalry's half-suspended breath.

Although like Sampson he was ta'en,
And by the base Philistines slain,
Yet he in death accomplished more
Than e'er he had in life before.
His noble heart, which ne'er had failed,
Proved firm, and e'en in death prevailed;
And many a tear drop dimmed the eye
Of e'en his foes who saw him die—
And none who witnessed that foul act
Will e'er in life forget the fact.

'Twas on a clear December day,
So mild it seemed, that gentle May
Had, in respect for that dread hour,
Donated one from her sweet bower.
No clouds were seen in all the sky,
Save one, and that was hovering nigh,
As though its mission was to screen
From angels' ken the awful scene.
For when upon the scaffold bare,
The hero stood, that cloud was there,
But when the throng pronounced him dead
That mystic cloud and screen had fled.

His lifeless form his friends besought,
And far, far from that wretched spot,
And from those scenes of suffering
To which such dreadful memories cling,
And to a freer, purer soil,
Uncursed by sweat of unpaid toil,
And to an unfrequented nook,
Whereon no craven eye may look,
Where Freedom doth her vigil keep,
They laid him down to dreamless sleep.

Scarce had his friend in calm repose
Entombed his form, when there arose
A restless spirit, which obtained,
Where e'er of liberty remained
A single spark of honest thought,
Too sacred to be sold or bought.
And thus the truths for which he died
Spread everywhere, and multiplied,
And rolled on like a foaming sea,
Until the Sons of Liberty
In all their majesty came forth,
And styled themselves the mighty North;
And from their ranks selected one,
An unassuming woodman's son,
Who bore their standard midst the feud,
And mighty contest which ensued.

He was from nature's plastic mold,
What kings and mighty men of old
Through lengthened years of toil, in vain
Had sought and striven to attain;
All that a language could express
Of noble-hearted faithfulness.
There was no grace he did not court,
Nor blemish in his manly port,
Tall, and of commanding form
And Heaven ordained to rule the storm.
There was a calm serenity,
    A kind, persuasive, artless art
Pervading the Divinity
    Which filled his great and manly heart.

All manly forms that graced his sight,
He deemed them men or black or white;
He bowed to all with deference,
And won a world of reverence.

He was that Son of Liberty,
Whose Heaven-approved fidelity
Made every act of his sublime.
And safely might we challenge Time,
With his deep, enveloped page,
The annals of a nameless age,
To bring forth one of purer mold,
Or one who had a stronger hold
Upon his country's throbbing heart,
Then he whose native, artless art
Has carved his own undying name
Upon the deathless scroll of fame.

Need I here that name pronounce,
Where if each heart would speak at once,
The glorious, grand response would be
"Lincoln, the friend of Liberty!"
If Fame's all glorious scroll were lost,
And there remained the merest ghost
Of all the present, of all the past,
If deathless liberty could last,
Her share of glory to receive,
Great Lincoln's name would also live!

———

BUT to return, when slavery's hosts
    Saw how that all their plans had failed,
And how that he, they envied most,
    Had e'en despite their wiles prevailed;
They grew incensed, and madly blind,
    And swore by all that had been done
To rend the sacred bands which bind
    Our many glorious states in one,—
And in their stead, build of their own
    A time enduring dynasty,

Whose spreading base and corner stone
  Should rest on *human slavery*.
To such an epoch they had bent,
  For thirty years their vulturous eye,
And well-provisioned the event,
  With every species of supply.
The arsenals were in their hands,
  And in their hands were all the spoil,
And all the soldiery of our lands
  Were rendezvousing on their soil,
With these unique advantages,
  And deeming their success as sure,
Like Hell-inspired savages
  Upon the nation's flag they pour
Volleys of grape and canister,
  Then seized the navy, and reversed
Its purpose, so as to deter
  The North, then dared them to their worst.

The news spread forth with speed of thought
  In all directions o'er the land;
Nor nook nor point was there forgot.
  It swept its length from strand to strand,
The State was like the storm-lashed sea,
  Chafing itself with wild unrest,
No bounds were there to the degree
  Of rage, apparent and expressed.
All business lay in blank suspense;
  And men stood idly here and there,
With no apparent deference
  To secular pursuit or care.

No ships of war, nor arms nor men,
  The treasury in a broken state;
And every *post a rebel den,*
  Where treason brawled in high debate,—

Is but a picture faintly drawn,
　Too faint by far except to cull
Some scattered fragments of the dawn
　Of Lincoln's first inaugural.

Now, as our chief executive,
　His first great office to perform
Was on the moment to conceive
　A means by which to check the storm,
Which soon would burst from its confines,
And sweep along our northern lines
With lightning flash and thunder roar,
More terrible than aught before.

He called for loyal men of war,
　Five and seventy thousand strong:
'Twas heralded anear and far,
　And answered by a mighty throng.
They came of every clime and race
　Of which our glorious land can boast,
With anxious hearts to take their place
　In freedom's cause at any post.

And some there came of Afric's hue,
　Though born and reared upon our shore,
Who eager were to don the blue,
　As they had done in days before.
As they had done at Lexington,
　At Bunker Hill and Brandywine,
At Monmouth and at Bennington,
　'Midst freedom's boasts in freedom's line.

As they had done at New Orleans,
　And on Lake Erie's troubled waves,
And in a word, 'midst all the scenes,
　Made sacred through our struggling braves.

But prejudice and foul disdain
  Rebuked and scorned their proffered aid,
And taunting, urged that slavery's chain
  Bore no relation to the raid.

And thus they grew, the jeer and butt
  Of the derisive and the vile;
And suffered many a cruel cut
  From rostrum and from press the while.
These prated of *a White Man's war,*
  And claimed that Negroes feared to die;
That face of those who placed the scar
  Upon their backs would make them fly.

Such was the feelings which possessed
  The loyal heart when Sumpter's fort
By rebel soldiers was distressed,
  And we could render no support.
And such the feeling which prevailed
  Up to our sad Bull Run retreat;
For ever yet our arms had failed
  The rebel forces to defeat.

Our dead lay bleaching on the plains,
  By scores of thousands slept they there,
While liberty, with plaintive strains,
  Was calling fresh recruits to war.
Our hospitals were running o'er
  With all our sick and wounded braves;
And in one line a thousand score
  Of stalwart, hail and idle slaves.

Of these their masters some were dead,
  And prisoners some, but all were foes,
Who from their slaves and homes had fled,
  The Union forces to oppose.

O Prejudice! thou art to blame
  For half of all the noble braves
Who fell in Freedom's sacred name;
  'Twas thy base deeds that dug their graves!

Witness thy truckling course, and then
Defer thy case to honest men;
To judge betwixt thy soul and mine.
Behold within the Union line
Scores of thousands of brawny arms
Held up in view of war's alarms,
Pulsating with their force of life,
And anxious for the scenes of strife,—
Anxious to wield the battle sword
'Gainst vile oppression's murderous horde,
Praying heaven, and praying earth
To grant them license to go forth,
And bear their part where freedom's braves
Were falling in untimely graves.

Alas! alas, their humble prayer
Fell heedless on the murky air,
And met no answer in return,
Except a cold and heartless spurn.
And yet, while thou wert scorning these,
Our forces, both by land and seas,
Were being worsted in the fight,
And pressed at times e'en unto flight,
Leaving behind their graveless dead,
And wounded braves, uncared or fed.

And yet thou hold'st at thy command,
Ready whereon to lay thy hand,
A hundred thousand stalwart blacks,
Eager to don their haversacks,

And rush with muskets to the field,
Or swords dissevered from their shield,
And there to pledge 'neath Heaven's blue sky
To conquer treason's host or die.
And yet they were denied the right—
Denied the privilege to fight
'Gainst rebels, who had veiled in gloom
Full many a Northern heart and home.

And wherefore were they thus denied
Until the glory and the pride
Of all our mighty North was taken
And lifeless strewn o'er many a plain?
Oh! Prejudice! thou art to blame
    For half of all the noble braves
Who fell in freedom's sacred name;
    'Twas thou, foul fiend, that dug their graves!

But for thy forked tongue of guile
Blood would have flowed not half the while;
But for thy craven heart of guilt
Not half the blood would have been spilt;
Yet, in despite thy rant and boast,
The right shall live when e'en thy ghost,
Thy hated ghost, thou cursed thing,
Shall to the drift of raiment cling!

*   *   *   *   *   *   *

The mission of the war was plain,
    But prejudice so dimmed our sight
That long we blindly strove in vain,
    Groping our way amidst the light.

The mission of the war was this—
  To force the bolt, unbar the door,
And let the long oppressed go free;
  It was no veiled hypothesis,
But plain, so plain that all might see,
  E'en to the poorest of the poor.

And some did see, and feigned they saw it not,
While others saw and cursed their hapless lot.
But those who long in darkness dwelt,
  And those who in death's shadow stood,
Saw its bright beams; they saw and felt,
  And well its purpose understood.

For straight they took their harps once more
  From off the boughs where they had hung,
And ran their stiffened fingers o'er
  Their chords, to which the moss had clung,
When lo! to their too great surprise,
  Those chords possessed their wonted glee
And chanted to the very skies
  The rising dawn of jubilee.

But those who dwelt upon the plain,
  Or sported on the mountain high,
When prejudice had left his stain,
  Saw no bright bow of promise nigh.

For we had sought to crush the South,
  Without the black man or his aid,
And to this end had taxed the North,
  And West and East to quell the raid,
And yet the rebels kept the field
  With reinforcements in reserve,
Before our troops they would not yield,
  Nor widely from their purpose swerve.

Full twenty moons had waxed and waned,
  And war had darkened many a home,
Before the anxious black obtained
  The right, a soldier to become.

But not till we had vainly tried
  To reconcile our traitorous foe:
Not until we, with humbled pride,
  Had really begged them to forego,

And e'en were driven to destroy
  Their institution of support,
Did we a single black employ,
  In rank or navy, field or fort.

But when the time had quite expired;
  The hundred days of the decree,
And God and justice now required
  The bondsman's promised liberty—

Then noble Lincoln, armed with might,
And clothed with honor, truth and right,
Stretched forth his hand, and took the quill,
  And tracing it along the page,
He framed, with heaven-admiring skill,
  The crowning feature of his age—

That God inspired instrument!
  Charter of manhood—Liberty!
Heaven ordained and heaven sent
  To rid our land of slavery!

The news thereof spread far and wide,
  And filled each humble slave's abode
With the grand and joyous tide
  Of blessings which had been bestowed.

Then wild the Union to assist,
    As regulars or volunteers,
The blacks rushed forward to enlist
    'Midst thunder shouts and deafening cheers.

Old Massachusetts' Fifty-fourth
    Filed into line, and swelled the ranks,
And charged so nobly on the South
    As to extort the Nation's thanks.

Then came the arming of the slaves,
    The noble Butler's "contrabands,"
Who proved themselves not only braves,
    But ranked the soldiers of our lands.

Then black men went as substitutes
    While timid white men staid at home;
Thus swelled the ranks of all recruits,
    Till bloody treason met its doom.

Two hundred thousand strong they stood,
    And fought for liberty and right,
And quite as freely shed their blood
    As those proud braves whose skins were white.

They bravely fought! And is that all
    That truth can say in their defense?
They drank the very dregs of gall,
    And bore a world of insolence.

And yet of Liberty's tried friends,
    They ranked the truest of the true;
Ne'er having swerved for selfish ends,
    Nor coupled treason with their hue.

For twelve score years in feeless toil,
    They labored for our country's good,
Delved in our mines, wrought on our soil,
    And fertilized our fields with blood.

In all our wars they bore their part,
    Nor shrank from dangers imminent,
Mingling the life-blood of their heart
    With that of braves most eminent.

And yet, through all those lengthened years,
    Their life was one of grief and pain,
And groans, and sighs, and bitter tears,
    And worse than all, a life of chains.

But there's to every day an eve,
    And unto every night a morn,
And joys there are for those who grieve,
    Howe'er dejected and forlorn!

The wrong may triumph for a while,
    But right comes uppermost at last,
And love shall bloom, and peace shall smile,
    When error's hated reign is past.

Lift up your hearts, ye long oppressed,
    And hail the gladsome rising dawn,
For Slavery's night, that sore distressed
    And tortured you, has passed and gone!

And Liberty's refulgent blaze
    Lights up our broad, unbroken land,
And nowhere 'neath her spreading rays
    Lives there a fetter or a brand!

All hail! the land has been redeemed
  From thraldom's foul and ruthless sway;
And Freedom's radiant light has streamed
  Along the bondman's gloomy way!

And in those dungeons of despair,
  Whence every ray of hope had fled,
Blest Liberty had entered there
  And breathed new life into the dead.

And o'er those regions of the brand,
  Where toil was recompensed with scorn,
Has waved abroad her flaming wand;
  And lo! a nation there is born—

And clothed upon with sacred rights;
  Those sacred rights of jealous care,
In whose defense the torch she lights,
  And strips her arm of vengeance bare.

O, Liberty! thou peerless queen!
  Thou quenchless essence of the soul,
Preside o'er these in every scene,
  And ward them 'gainst all base control;

Plant in their hearts a love of thought,
  An anxious spirit to acquire
Those mighty truths that are only bought
  With perseverance and desire.

Move them to grasp with hand and heart,
  And with a deathless will beside,
Each mode of science, skill and art,
  Consistent with our Nation's pride:

So that the world may ne'er regret
　The mighty work that's been performed,
And so that Time his seal may set
　Upon their future all adorned.

　　*　　*　　*　　*　　*　　*　　*

There is no right a freeman has
　So purely sacred as his choice.
How e'er bereft he'll cling to this,
　And in its potency rejoice:

For in its exercise he stands
　The peer of titled wealth and state,
How e'er possessed of spreading lands,
　Or gifted they in high debate—

He is their peer, however grand,
　Or much upon themselves they dote,
For there's no station in our land
　Which ranks a man above his vote.

The right to exercise a right;
　The right to choose 'twixt man and man;
The *right* to battle for the right,
　And in the right do what we can,

Is manhood clothed with liberty—
　The just, inherent right of all,
Regardless of ability,
　Or age, or sex, or great or small!

That right today the black man wields
　With gratitude, though long denied,
For deep within his heart he feels
　A sacredness of joy and pride.

Nobly the war has done its work,
　　And nobly the Republicans,
With no apparent wish to shirk,
　　Have canceled Freedom's high demands.

They took the fetters in their hand,
　　And wrenched them from the bleeding limb;
Then took the slave 'neath their command,
　　And nurtured and disciplined him.

They gave subsistence to his wife,
　　And to his little ones gave bread,
And thus amid the scenes of strife
　　Were countless thousands clothed and fed.

They formed the Freedmen's Bureau Bill,
　　Which placed the letter in his hand,
And gave him schools, despite the will
　　Of him, the tyrant, in command.

They framed the Bill of Civil Rights,
　　By which his living was secured
Against those vile malevolent whites
　　Whose souls to treason were inured.

Then toward our fundamental laws
　　They bent their hearts in zealous toil,
And thereunto affixed a clause
　　Which banished slavery from our soil.

This nobly done, they still propose
　　Our charter further to amend,
By making citizens of those
　　The law had proffered to defend.

Though 'twas a grave step in the right,
　　The party claimed it none the less,
And girding well their loins with might,
　　They fought the issue to success.

This contest, proudly fought and won,
　　Left one just claim uncanceled yet,
Before the world-wide shout, well done!
　　Would ring from freedom's minaret.

To council this, the final claim,
　　And merit freedom's grand applause,
And win a fadeless wreath of fame,
　　Through noble deeds in manhood's cause;
They concentrated all their might,
　　Which great Ulysses deigned to lead?
And claimed the *Franchise* as a right,
　　And just investment of the freed.

To every State went forth the claim,
　　How e'er convenient or remote,
And everywhere, in freedom's name,
　　They pressed the freedman's right to vote.

State after State endorsed the fact,
　　Which lent new ardor to their zeal—
A zeal which no incentive lacked
　　To strengthen or enforce appeal.

Full thirty States at length filed out,
　　And proudly stood on manhood's side;
And Freedom raised the joyous shout,
　　"Well done! All hail! All satisfied!"

This was the crowning act of all;
  And placed upon one common base,
Of all this mighty rolling ball
  A specimen of every race.

Freedom's proud temple's now complete,
  Crowned with the long-rejected stone;
And we are here to hail and greet
  The master minds by which 'twas done.

Hail! Master Workmen, noble band!
  And hail the key-stone, and the arch,
The pride and glory of our land!
  And hail, to manhood's onward march!

The night of gloom, the night of sorrow,
  The night of wrong, the night of chains,
At length has passed, and lo! the morrow
  Of joy has dawned, and Freedom reigns.

For, in our nation's Senate Hall,
  A Negro has his seat today,
Where, e'en in memory's brief recall,
  Sat Calhoun, Webster, Cass and Clay.

Rejoice, O land, bought by the sword,
  Redeemed and by the sword set free!
Let all thy sons, with one accord,
  Be jubilant o'er thy victory.

That we should have a member, where
  One decade back, 'twere worth the head
Of such as he, to even dare
  Within those sacred halls to tread,

Proves that the world doth surely move,
    And proves that men of worth may rise
From low estate, and soar above
    Their former selves in nature's guise.

How wondrous the coincident,
    That from the Great Arch Rebel's home,
His erring State to represent,
    Our first Black Senator should come,
A seat of office to complete,
    Made vacant through Jeff's recreancy.
O, for the privilege to greet
That Negro in that Rebel's seat!
    'Twere worth the distance and expense.

But this is not the only post
By Negroes filled, deserving boast:
We have a Judge upon the seat,
    And Ministers in foreign lands,
At home, a Governor, to greet,
    And Legislators e'en in bands.

The prayed-for time has come at last—
    The time of which we used to sing,
The good time talked of in the past,
    Is here today upon its wing—
The ballot's in the black man's hand;
    Promotion waits him at his door,
And peace and plenty crown our land,
    And freedom reigns from shore to shore.

Strike all your bells, ye lofty spires!
    Wave all your banners, freedom wave!
Loose your tongues, ye tell-tale wires,
    And you, ye thundering cannons rave!

America, the land of science,
    The land of every nation's love,
Has formed with Freedom an alliance
    So pure, 'tis registered above!

Lift up your heads, ye lofty mountains!
    Clap your glad hands, ye mighty seas!
Leap for joy, ye crystal fountains,
    And odors waft sweet balmy breeze!
The crowning work is now accomplished,
    The builders have received the stone!
Dark Slavery's fame has been demolished,
    And all his Dagon gods o'erthrown!

And on its base a mighty temple,
    Gorgeous, grand, sublime and free!
O'er whose proud dome and lofty steeple
    Presides eternal Liberty!

Stand proudly up, aged sire!
    Be filled with hope, elastic boy;
Bring forth the lute and tune the lyre,
    And let us have a feast of joy!

For lo! the hand that held the musket,
    And strangled treason in the fight,
Has laid aside the war-worn corselet,
    And taken the ballot as a right!

And the right at his discretion
    To wield it as his faith may guide
Responsible for each digression,
    To God, his country, and his pride!

And now, in conclusion, accept a brief line
Inscribed to *our* country, thy country and mine.

Hail! hail mighty Land with thy proud destiny!
Enduring as time, all chainless and free!
Hail! hail to thy mountains majestic and high,
Reclining their heads against the blue curtained
    sky.

And hail to thy valleys so fragrant and fair,
With wild flowers blooming and scenting the air,
And hail to thy prairies, outspreading and wide,
Resembling the Ocean's broad billowless tide.

And hail to thy Streamlets, all wending their way
Adown to their Rivers, more mighty than they;
And hail to thy Rivers as onward they sweep
Through th' low valley lands to their home in the
    deep;

And hail to thy Oceans, all dotted with sails,
Their white wings extended, inviting the gales;
And hail to thy Commerce, the pride of the world,
And hail to thy Standard so proudly unfurled;

And hail to thy Cities all teaming with life,
Where the interest of all is the center of strife.
And hail to thy Railroads and steam-driven trains,
That sweep through thy mountains and dash o'er
    thy plains;

And hail to thy Telegraph, thy glory and prime,
Defying all distance, and outstripping Time,
Extending its arms through the heart of the sea
And binding all Realms to the Land of the Free;

And hail to thy Magistrates, Judges and Courts,
And Armies and Navies, thy strength and sup-
 ports.

And hail to thy Congress, where thy statesmen
 are met,
Where thy wisdom for ages in Counsel have sat.
And hail to thy Chief, the Bright Crown of thy
 State,
The gallant Ulysses, all glorious and great;

And hail, once again, thy glory and pride,
Bright Banner of Freedom, out-spreading and
 wide.

There's not a dark spot on thy features today,
As pure as the heavens, and radiant as they;
Thus, ever proud Banner, exultingly wave,
Thou glory and pride of the unfettered slave.

Poem.

In commemoration of the death of Abraham
Lincoln, delivered at the great public meeting
of colored citizens on Tuesday evening, April
18, 1865, Sacramento, Cal.

Wherefore half-mast and waving sadly
    And seeming ill-disposed to move,
    Are those bright emblems which so
       gladly
    Were wont to wave our homes above?
And why is all this lamentation?
    And why those outward signs of woe?
And why is this all-glorious nation
    Thus in her hour of hope bowed low?

Wherefore those marks of grief and sorrow
    So visible on every face?
To what foul deed of bloody horror
    Do all those gloomy signs retrace?
Aback to the walls and lofty spire!
    Back to the Nation's Halls of State!
Back to our country's bleeding sire!
    Back to our dying Magistrate!

We know not why God has permitted
    This tragic scene, this bloody deed;
An act so seemingly unfitted,
    In this auspicious hour of need.
Though none perhaps may the intention,
    Or the wonderous purpose tell,
Of this direful life-suspension—
    Yet God, the Lord, doeth all things well!

Our Nation's Father has been murdered!
  Our Nation's Chieftain has been slain!
By traitorous hands most basely ordered;
  And we, his children, feel the pain.
Our pain is mixed with indignation,
  Our sorrow is not purely grief,
And nothing short of a *libation*
  From *Treason's* heart can bring relief.

And we, in sight of earth and heaven,
  On bended knee, with lifted hand,
Swear as we hope to be forgiven,
  To drive foul Treason from the land!
And that fair land so long polluted
  By the sweat of unpaid toil,
Shall be by liberty uprooted,
  And thickly spread with freedom's soil.

Thus we'll avenge the death of Lincoln,
  His noble principles maintain,
Till every base inhuman falcon
  Is swept from freedom's broad domain;
Until from tower and from turret,
  From mountain height and prairie wide,
One flag shall wave—and freedom's spirit
  In peace and love o'er all preside.

The Future of America, in the Unity of the Races.

Respectfully dedicated to

BISHOP BENJAMIN W. ARNETT,

A life-long and devoted friend and a noble and loyal citizen whose work for God and the good of the race is bearing its fruits, presenting to the present generation of colored youth an inspiring example for their honest, earnest, individual effort.

Once in a time along the Jordan,
 And e'en from Beersheba to Dan,
The question rife and all-absorbing
 Hither and thither wildly ran,
 What think you of this Christ, this
 Jesus?
What of his intercourse with man?
The which to solve full many a thesis
Has been the sport of mind and pen.

But we today would feign a question
 Bring home to each American;
No deep-veiled, mystified suggestion,
 But simply, what think you of man?
Not of the angels high and holy,
 Not of the streets of shining gold,
Nor of the doomed in hades lowly,
 Nor of time, with his step so bold.

These were themes for speculation,
  On which the mind might cogitate
And weary e'en imagination,
  With heights, and depths, and breadth so great.
But what of man, is he thy brother,
  In all his variableness of hue?
And is thy God and God thy Father,
  Alike his God and Father, too?

Is he entitled and deserving
  In all that's common to the race,
Whether in ruling or in serving,
  Adjudged by fitness in the case?
These are the questions of the hour,
  And these the issues of the day;
On these the wisdom, skill and power
  Of this great nation deigns to play.

For here, not only the religion,
  But each man's patriot faith and creed,
Will blazen forth in his decision
  Till even he that runs may read.
Therefore, let him within whose nature
  An impulse lives, though weak, to do
Aright by every living creature,
  Cherish that impulse and be true—

True to a grand and generous manhood;
  True to the spirit of the age,
Whose motto is untrammeled selfhood
  For human life in every stage,
And on this heaven-established basis
  Whoever builds near need not make haste,
For coming freedman's glorious trace,
  Too radiant are to be defaced.

Too high within the mortal heaven
  Has risen the star of destiny,
And far too wide has spread the leaven
  Of freedom and equality.
We may not with a will concede it,
  As from the fullness of our hearts,
But freedman's God has thus decreed it,
  And the boon we must impart.

No combined power of human effort
  Can turn the joyous time aside,
Laden with fruits of hope and comfort
  To anxious millions long denied.
As well confront the mighty ocean,
  Lashing with rage his rock-bound shores,
And strive to curb his wild commotion,
  Or drown the thunder of his roar,
As to resist the coming morrow
  Which liberty, and truth, and God
Have promised these dark sons of sorrow
  So long enchained and 'neath the rod.

Must we put forth our vain endeavors
  And waste our efforts on the wind,
And learn too late that mortals never
  Can change what heaven has designed?
We may provoke God's indignation,
  And cause the heavens again to frown,
Till his avenging visitations
  Cause us in sorrow to bow down,
Yet on and on will sweep the current,
  Now putting in from Freedom's sea,
Rushing onward like a torrent,
  Flooding the land with liberty.

We may attempt to drive them from us,
 Beyond the confines of our shore,
For even now are there among us
 Monsters with thoughts so vile in store.

But dare we do it, these jester's slave-men,
 Poor dupes of unrequitted toil,
When we can no longer deprave them,
 Drive them to other lands, the spoil
Of a miasma wildly raging
 Beneath an endless summer's sun,
Where listless sloth has been enslaving
 The mind of man since time begun?

Dare we do this, and righteous heaven
 Pour out on us new vials of wrath,
Until our land, all rent and riven,
 Shall welter in a crimson bath?
Oh, stand in awe of God's displeasure;
 Our sure destruction we may buy,
And through our baseness fill the measure
 Of our guilt, and cursed of heaven die.

The means of life and self destruction
 Are placed in every nation's reach,
While error, the bane of reproduction,
 Insinuates at every breach.
Beware! If God has built this nation
 All its constituents are good
And needful to its preservation,
 Whether they be stone or wood.

We may not comprehend the structure
 In full minutial design,
Nor trace its varied architecture
 In arris, groove, and curve, and line.

Be but faithful, and the Great Grand Master
   Will on his trestle board make plain
All that's obtuse, but no whit faster
   Than 'twere needful to explain.

But can we not perceive a purpose
   In the peopling of this land,
Destined of God to be the foremost
   And the grandest of the grand?
And have we not beheld the nations
   In spreading o'er the vastly sphere,
That as they spread them weaker traces
   Of their varied types appear?
There is a principle in nature,
   And demonstrative everywhere,
Inanimate and breathing creature,
   The self-established truth declare;

All branches of the common center
   Diminish and weaken in their course,
The germ in every part doth enter,
   But ever with abated force.
Behold the oak with spreading branches,
   The trunk-life lives in every branch,
But as in length each limb advances
   It loses strength and sustenance.
The giant oak's unbroken forces
   Within no single branch is found,
And faultless nature ne'er reverses
   This law in all her varied round.

The huge oak's branches, closely blended
   And all completely unified,
Would rival all the force expended,
   And varied life so long supplied.

Turn to those early peopled regions—
To Europe, Asia, Africa:
The home of science and religions,
And tell us what of them today?
Where now is all their former glory?
And where that grandeur and renown
That radiates the page of story,
As diamond jettings doth a crown?

Where now their sculptors and their sages,
Their painters and their orators?
And where the pride of all the ages—
Their poets and philosophers?
Where now the minds that planned their temples,
The proud Colossus reared at Rhodes,
Grand architectural examples
And ever-living sculptural modes?
Their day of grandeur has departed;
Their sun of glory has gone down,
And passed away the valiant hearted,
Their mighty men of great renown.

Their wondrous temples are in ruins,
Apollo sleeps beneath the sea;
For time has here wrought sad undoings
And carved on all degeneracy.
The branch had here become too distant
From the great Adamic tree,
And hence the germ and life assistant
Had grown too meagre in degree;
For where man lives in isolation,
Though vast possessions he embrace,
As family, tribe, kingdom or nation,
Degeneracy has marked the race.

Hence, while the clannish tribes were sweeping
    The wide-spread east in their unrest,
Heaven for a glorious end was keeping
    In blest reserve the mighty west;
But not until their wasted powers
    Gave evidence of sure decay,
Was this wealth-flowing land of ours
    Thrown in a wandering seaman's way,
Wherein a branch of every nation
    And tongue and tribe beneath the sun,
Should spend the days of their probation
    And finally converge into one—

One, wherein the scattered forces
    Of the great Adamic tree,
With all its varied life resources,
    Should blend in perfect harmony.
And by that unifying process,
    Give earth once more a glorious type
Of wisdom, grace and noble prowess
    Co-equal with the architype;

A genius of a new creation,
    Whom all shall hail with loud acclaim,
Whose boast shall be a blood relation
    To all the kindred sons of fame.
Toward this seeming innovation
    Point all the dial hands of fate,
And to its final consummation
    On fleeting Time's revolving plate.

It may be years, it may be ages,
    The finale is with God alone,
Who measures not by dates and pages,
    But by the fiat of his throne;

For in the near or distant future
  Of all those tribal branches here,
Scarce aught will live in speech or feature
  Of what their great ancestors were.

For with the unity of branches
  Will come a unity of speech,
Correcting old and groundless fancies
  Discordant tongues could never reach.

Dependent are we on each other
  And parts essential to a whole,
Strive as we may this fact to smother,
  The truth will brook all vain control.

One man, Jehovah, God created,
  In whom all graces did combine,
To whom earth's myriads are related,
  E'en as the branch is to the vine.

And as the thrifty vine while growing
  Round distant limbs its fibers twine,
With all its wealth of shade bestowing,
  Comprises but a single vine.

So, in the light of heaven's deeming,
  Whose broad eye doth creation span
Earth's tribes in all their varied seeming,
  Combine to form a single man.

We are not independent creatures;
  Our brothers' keepers are we all,
Bearing the likeness and the features
  Of God, our Maker, great and small;

Though darker than the shades of blackness,
  Or fairer than the morning light,
It matters not, in strict exactness,
  God's image are we, black or white.

The inspirations of our natures,
  Declare to us, though erring creatures,
Of each we are integral parts.
  Then here, where fortune has assigned us,
'Neath God's blue dome of liberty,
  Let deathless bands of friendship bind us
In bonds of blest fidelity,
  That in the future grand unfolding,
When all our dark, perplexing fears,
  Respecting rights and their withholding,
Are buried in the grave of years,
  Man shall arise in all his grandeur,
In all his native dignity,
  And go forth daring fear or danger,
The ward of peace and liberty.

The Youthful Villager and the Hermit.

Once on a clear autumnal day,
    With weary heart and spirit bowed,
I sought a silent scene away
    From all the turmoil of the crowd.

And where a rent primeval rock
    Reared high its head o'er spire and dome,
Which seemed majestic and to mock
    The structure of my plebeian home.

I bent in gaze my straining eye,
    And yielding to a transient freak,
Resolved within my soul to try
    And scale the towering cloud-capped peak.

What tiresome moments, more or less,
    I toiled in gaining half its height,
When lo! a shadowy, deep recess
    Allured and filled me with delight.

And turning from my onward march
    I found it easy of access,
And passing 'neath a rural arch,
    I gained a scene of loveliness.

It might have been a warrior's home,
    The home of chiefs who dealt in scars,
Its walls were antique and its dome
    Was flaming with a thousand stars.

I scanned its countless beauties o'er,
  And turning from a scene too grand,
I passed again its arching door
  And gazed upon my own loved land.

I saw beneath, amid the throng,
  The poor man subject to the proud;
And while I thought of right and wrong,
  I, all forgetting, thought aloud.

Till then, alas; I little knew
  Of man's inhuman acts to man,
But from that panoramic view
  I, half complaining, thus began:

"If there were less of selfishness,
  If friends were less untrue;
How much of all earth's wretchedness
  Would vanish from our view.

The rich man then would cease to grind
  The fate of him that's poor;
And soon the wretch, and wandering hind
  Would vanish from our door.

And if the stream of kindness ran
  More freely through the heart,
Then, erring man would feel for man
  And act a brother's part;

The golden rule he would obey,
  And seek the poor man's cot;
And with his kindly aid assay
  To change his hapless lot.

For there's enough for every one;
 Enough, and some to spare.
Enough of comforts 'neath the sun
 For all that breathe to share.

Were only half that's vainly spent
 To make an empty show,
Amid the haunts of sorrow sent,
 'Twould heal a world of woe.

And oh! how fragrant would become
 Each balmy breath of morn,
If every hovel was a home,
 And there were none forlorn.

As fair as Eden's blooming grove,
 Would this sad world appear;
If man to man would only prove,
 In all his acts, sincere.

But man! oh, selfish, sordid man!
 How like a fiend at heart,
Deep skilled in every wily plan,
 He plays a demon's part.

See him exulting in his might
 Of pageantry and pride,
Passing unmoved amid the blight
 Of hunger unsupplied.

The orphan's cry for charity;
 The widow's lonely moan,
Awakes no chord of sympathy
 Within his heart of stone.

Although his basket and his store
  Have plenty in supply,
He doth unto the aged poor
  A crust of bread deny.

O Thou! the source of every cause
  In air, and earth, and sea!
Whose ceaseless and unerring laws
  Move all in harmony;

Why do thy gifts to man on earth
  Unequal still appear?
Why go some toiling from their birth,
  E'en to their graves in fear?

While others, decked in fine array,
  Drink deep at pleasure's court,
And pass this life as but a day,
  In idle glee and sport!

Why do the thousands starve and thirst,
  And others die of cold?
And last of all, and still the worst,
  Why are the millions sold?

Perchance there lies some latent good
  Beyond my feeble ken,
By angels seen and understood,
  But not perceived by men.

Yet why should not the culprit know
  Wherefore he stands arraigned?
Why should the expiating blow
  Fall on him unexplained?

Fain would we hope in Adam's fall
  To have seen the problem solved;
But find alas! his guilt for all
  In life's great cup dissolved.

For of one blood all men were made,
  To dwell in all the earth;
And Adam's sin was shared and laid
  At each man's door at birth.

Condemned to toil were all the race;
  But is it thus with all?
The gilded idler struts apace
  Mid rank and pomp and ball.

Then, oh! from whence hath man the power,
  The absolute control,
To play the mock-god for an hour
  O'er human heart and soul?"

*   *   *   *   *   *   *

The sun had rolled his golden car
  Adown behind the western hill;
And I, amid the rocks afar,
  Stood wrapped in meditation still.

While o'er the landscape far and near
  A greyish, sombre veil had spread,
Suggesting to the soul the drear
  And awful silence of the dead.

Fair Cynthia with her smiling face,
  And all her diamond-spangled train,
Were pouring from the fields of space
  Their silver beams o'er hill and plain.

Just as I turned to leave the scene
  And seek again my humble cot,
I spied a man with hoary mien,
  The hermit of some lonely grot.

"Be not in haste," said he, "young man;
  Thy task is incomplete.
In quest of truth thou oughtest scan
  Beneath the surface sheet.

And that thine age may ne'er undo
  The labors of thy youth,
Learn this, no superficial view
  Hath e'er revealed a truth.

There is a source for every stream,
  A cause for every woe,
But veiled in mist they often seem
  To mortals here below.

Canst thou behold yon silvery moon
  And all the stars above,
And still the omniscient God impugn
  With motives less than love?

Those stars are worlds, for aught we know,
  And peopled like our own;
And move and live within the glow
  And presence of God's throne.

For earth is but a speck of sand
  Compared to all the spheres
That ushered from Jehovah's hand
  When time began his years.

And canst thou think! Ah, think again!
   Canst thou believe that he
The God of all yon starry train,
   Would work thy misery?

But thou wouldst know why wrongs abound,
   And whence man hath the power
To crush his fellow to the ground,
   And like a beast, devour.

Thou mayst find in Adam's fall
   A key for every 'why,'
Of blood and want and woe, with all
   The wrongs beneath the sky.

For man, the last and crowning sheaf,
   The sixth day's work of Heaven,
Was made by God, and crowned a chief,
   And wide dominion given.

Made like his God, God of his will,
   With reason for his guide,
And power to choose the good or ill,
   Or either cast aside.

Thus crowned was he when first he trod
   Fair Eden's vale and wood,
And wore the image of his God,
   And God pronounced him good.

Good was the earth and all its bowers,
   Good every cool retreat;
And all the birds and beasts and flowers
   With goodness were replete."

The elements were all at rest,
  And tranquil as the rill,
No storm disturbed old Ocean's breast,
  His waves lay hushed and still,

No rattling thunder rolled on high,
  No forked lightning flew,
No blackening clouds obscured the sky,
  Nor angry storm winds blew ;

But when the impious hand of man
  Plucked, the forbidden tree,
Rebellion, through creation ran,
  Like electricity.

Old ocean's waves began to roll,
  And beasts on beasts, began to prey ;
Until, from pole to pole,
  Spread discord and dismay,

Sweet peace and love, on that dread morn
  Gave place to sad unrest,
And hate, became with pride and scorn,
  The tennants of the breast.

Since then till now, mankind like elves
  Have spurned all Heaven's decrees,
And preying on their sordid selves ;
  Wrought all earth's miseries.

Good and only good young friend,
  Has God, thy Maker, given,
But man, because he could offend
  And change to Hell, a Heaven—

Has seared his heart 'gainst every wail,
    And wreathed his brow with scorn,
Till pity's prayer hath no avail,
    And thousands die forlorn.

He bowed his head, he spake no more,
    And ere I'd thanked him for his care,
He darted 'neath his arching door,
    And left me lone, and lonely there.

Then cautiously, I clambered down,
    Assisted by fair Luna's light,
And when I gained my cot, and town,
    Lo, 'twas the silent noon of night.

Triumphs of the Free.

Hail, thou observed of many lands,
　　Let all thy banners be unfurled,
　This brilliant act of thine commands
　　The commendations of the world;
　And all the brave of every tongue
Shall heap encomiums on thy name,
While many a lute shall there be strung
To chant the wonders of thy fame.

No victory won by land or sea,
　No battle fought since war began,
Has done so much for liberty—
　So much for humanizing man—
And never, while that old flag waves,
　Proud ensign of the noble free,
Wilt thou achieve for all thy braves
　A more ennobling victory.

For lo! the lightning spark which flew
　With thought-like speed from east to west,
Brought to the honest, good, and true,
　Glad tidings—while to the oppressed
And writhing bondsman 'neath the yoke,
　It was as when o'er Bethlehem's plains
An angel-choir the silence broke,
　And charmed the shepherds with their strains.

To them, poor, hopeless, and forlorn,
　It seemed a Savior had been given—
A very Jesus had been born,
　The gift of God—a child of heaven.

For all the hopes of all their race,
  Swung on the slender thread of choice,
But interposing heavenly grace
  Controlled events, hence we rejoice.

Rejoice! rejoice! the bondsmen's free,
  The last foul link in their last chain,
This glorious Union victory
  Will change to molten ore again.
Rejoice! rejoice! our prayer's been heard;
  Let all who love the truth rejoice,
For lo! the man our hearts preferred
  Becomes again the nation's choice.

Her choice to fill that high estate,
  Grand place of trust, most lofty sphere,
Commandant and chief magistrate
  O'er all her interest far and near;
Her choice, but not from blood or birth,
  Or vague hereditary claim;
But chosen by the mighty North
  For honest truth and patriot fame!

Chosen because he loved this land,
  Dear home of his progenitors—
Too well to countenance a band
  Of traitorous conspirators;
Too well to see that noble flag,
  Beneath whose folds his fathers fought,
Insulted as a worthless rag,
  And thrust beneath the earth to rot.

Chosen again, though not as when
  The nation only deemed him true;
For now since all the skill of men
  Combined with treason's dastard crew.

In vain for four long years have tried
  His god-like truth to compromise,
He's grown a struggling nation's pride
  Whom millions love and idolize.

Whom millions love—why should they not?
  And though they verge idolatry,
When we compare their present lot
  With that of chains and slavery,
We scarcely can prefer a charge,
  'Tis so in keeping with the race
That whence they draw in blessings large,
  Thither their hearts best loves we trace.

But what had Lincoln done for those—
  Those weltering 'neath the gory rod?
Who through their chains and cruel blows,
  Had long been looking up to God?
This hath he done, by Truth's control,
  Gave Earth and Heaven the blest decree,
Which though it fail to reach the soul,
  Has rent the veil of Slavery.

Surely the gods have interposed,
  And surely heaven has answered prayer,
Else why are mercy's doors unclosed;
  And why this seeming special care;
And why this steady onward march
  Of Justice, Truth and Liberty;
And why doth heaven's o'er-spreading arch
  Look down with such complacency?

And why this overwhelming vote
  By which great Lincoln's been retained,
Whose wondrous acts of world-wide note
  Bears freedom to the long enchained?

God grant to him an arm of strength
Co-equal to his mighty heart;
Then shall our bleeding land at length
Bloom like the rose in every part.

To whom save him could we commit
The nation's weal till strife is closed,
And feel that he, in every whit,
Was equal to the task imposed?
Or, taking all our ills in view,
Together with this fiendish war,
Of all our noble heroes, who
Would we exchange our Lincoln for?

There's valiant Sherman, Grant and Sigel,
Each have bright laurels from the field,
For which of them could we our legal
Claim upon our faithful Lincoln yield?
Believe it, ye who will or may,
Of all earth's millions there are none
For whom America today
Would change her honest woodman's son.

He stands pre-eminently high,
With her the first of living men,
And at his will her warriors fly
To beard Secessia in his den.
And not until the monster lay
As docile as a crouching cur,
Would he command those braves away,
Urged on by each incentive spur.

But ere his office shall expire,
Or he its onerous tasks resign,
May Slavery die, and War retire,
And six and thirty States combine,

And blend in one unbroken Union,
　Based on the equal rights of man,
Where discontent or vain delusion
　Shall ne'er unsheath their swords again.

————

What Shall We Do With the Contrabands?

Shall we arm them?　Yes, arm them!
　　Give to each man
　　A rifle, a musket, a cutlass or sword;
　　Then on to the charge! let them war in
　　　the van,
　Where each may confront with his merciless
　　lord,
And purge from their race, in the eyes of the
　　brave,
The stigma and scorn now attending the slave.

I would not have the wrath of the rebels to cease,
　Their hope to grow weak nor their courage to
　　　wane,
Till the contrabands join in securing a peace,
　Whose glory shall vanish the last galling chain,
And win for their race an undying respect
In the land of their prayers, their tears and
　neglect.

Is the war one for Freedom?　Then why, tell me,
　　　why,
　Should the wronged and oppressed be debarred
　　from the fight?

Does not reason suggest, it were noble to die
  In the act of supplanting a wrong for the
    right?
Then lead to the charge! for the end is not far,
When the contraband host are enrolled in the
    war.

"Liberty or Death."

Virginius, the Roman Father,
    With beating heart, though brave,
  Beheld his fair Virginia doomed,
    To be a tyrant's slave.

Despair had gather'd on his brow,
    Commingled with regret;
  A gleam of hope ran through his soul,
    I may redeem her yet.

Come hither, belov'd Virginia,
    Ere we forever part;
  He clasp'd her to his beating breast,
    Then stab'd her to the heart.

Thus, did a Roman Father slay,
    The idol of his soul,
  To screen her from a tyrant's lust,
    A tyrant's foul control.

Though this was done in days of yore,
　　The act was truly brave;
What value, pray, is life to man,
　　If that man be a slave?

Go and ask of Margaret Garner,
　　Who's now in prison bound,
(No braver woman e'er hath trod,
　　Columbia's slave-cursed ground:)

Why did she with a mother's hand
　　Deprive her child of breath?
She'll tell you, with a Roman's smile,
　　That slavery's worse than death.

O! that every bondman now,
　　Through all that slave-cursed land,
Had each a heart like Margaret's,
　　Their freedom to demand.

Then the Jubilee year would come;
　　On spire and dome you'd see
Inscribed in blazing characters,
　　That all mankind are free.

Long live the name of Margaret,
　　In every freeman's breast;
And when her days are numbered here,
　　May she in heaven be blest!

A Holy Messenger.

Dedicated to Rev. Thomas M. D. Ward.

The voice of Macedonia's gone
  From California o'er the seas,
And yet, to help her, there was none;
  No, none that offered to appease
Her anguish, and with words of cheer,
A cordial bring for all her fear.

At length that voice fell on thy heart,
  And yielding to its plaintive strain,
I see thee with thy kindred part—
  Resolved to cross the dashing main,
And plant life's crimson banner, where
Sin's dark pollutions taint the air.

Then all thy life, or short or long—
  Then all thy powers, small or great,
To God, to whom they all belong,
  Anew thou didst them dedicate;
And o'er the broad and trackless deep
Came hither both to sow and reap.

Thy coming found us poor indeed,
  Unsheltered from the blasts that blow,—
No sacred Zion where in need,
  Earth's sad and sorrowing ones might go;
And leave this world of care and doubt,
With all its carking fears without.

Thou didst not come as many came,
  Alone to fill thy purse with gold,
Thy mission and thy noble aim,
  God's glorious Gospel to unfold,
And through His aid, to seek and save
The lost and wrecked on ruin's wave.

Hence, with thy cross of faith upreared,
  Thy book of promise widely spread;
While godless thousands scoffed and jeered,
  Thou didst portray the life Christ led,
And how he bore sin's chastening rod
To win the erring back to God.

Though many scoffed, yet some gave heed;
  Though many scorned, yet some have prayed,
And found in that dread hour of need
  Thy Christ, their refuge and their aid;
Their friend, while passing through that vale
Where all our mortal friendship fail.

And thus thy labors have been crowned—
  Crowned with many a signal good;
While error's hosts have darkly frowned,
  Many have joined the angelhood;
And in life's morn, for each of them,
A star shall deck thy diadem.

Meanwhile thy toils have reared on high,
  In grand memorial of thy name,
Our bethel, where, as years sweep by,
  Shall live the record of thy fame—
The record of thy godly zeal,
That all may see, and know, and feel.

And now that duty calls thee hence,
  Once more to cross the briny wave,
Once more to stand in our defense,
  Amidst the holy, loved and brave;
Go, and may his presence be thy stay,
Whom maddening waves and winds obey.

Sons of Erin.

e sons of Erin who have come
    To this fair land to make your home,
    Look back upon your native shore,
    Where lordling rule makes thousands
          poor,
And tell me why ye stand arrayed
With those, who would your rights invade?
With those who would extend a course
Of human bondage, tenfold worse
Than England's Land Monopoly,
All o'er this land of Liberty.

Know ye not that with the class,
Known as the Democratic mass,
Stand your uncompromising foes,
And source of all our country's woes?
Tyrants, whose avaricious lust,
Would fain have ground you to the dust,
Long ere time's dial marked this hour,
Had their best wishes been their power.

Remember great O'Connell's name!
And sully not his world-wide fame
By any glaring act of shame;
Remember, how he once returned
To Southern planters moneys, earned
By the bondman 'neath the yoke,
And all those burning words he spoke;
And let your great example be
His life and marked consistency.

Eliza Harris' Parental Love.

When February's chilling winds
    Swept through the forest glen,
And nothing, save the smoking hut,
    Marked the abodes of men,
I through my lattice chanced to peep;
    And far amid the storm
A slender female shape advanced
    With something in her arms.

An unexpected sight like this
    Won my attention o'er,
And wistfully I stood, till she
    Rapped lightly at the door.
She entered, bearing in her arms
    A little sportive boy,
Whose jetty locks, though all disheveled,
    Revealed a face of joy.

Can I be ferried o'er the stream?
  Sad news I've heard of late
About one of my children, sir,
  I'm fearful of his fate.
She spoke this so imploringly
  That loath I felt to say,
The perils of the ice-gorged stream
  I cannot brave today.

At length I said, if possible
  Most freely I would go,
The floating ice is so condensed
  The boat cannot pass through.
'Twas evening, and the sun sank fast
  Toward the western mound,
And ere an hour could have past
  Night's gloom would spread around.

She lay her babe upon the bed
  And threw her bonnet by,
Then from the center of the soul
  Came one despairing sigh.
The tramp of horses' feet was heard
  Upon the frozen ground.
She stood aghast, then seized her child
  And made a fearful bound.

'Tis he, 'tis he, she wildly cried,
  Oh! save my darling child;
While towards the water's edge she ran
  Like one far more than wild.
She saw the tyrant pressing hard,
  Her Harry was his slave;
She then resolved to cross the stream
  Or perish 'neath the wave.

From slab to slab of floating ice
　　She leaped amid its roar,
Till with her Harry in her arms
　　She reached the other shore.
While he, who caused this fearful scene,
　　Stood speechless as a plank,
And saw the object of his chase
　　Borne safely up the bank.

She's free, and nobly has she won
　　The boon by nature given.
May she be blest while here on earth,
　　And doubly blest in heaven.

The First of August.

Hail! hail thou glorious first!
  Proud day of Liberty,
Thy dawning wakes the burst
  Of India's jubilee;
And calls to mind that happy morn
When Freedom's thousand sons were born.

That morn, when o'er the main
  Bless'd Freedom's angel flew,
And rent each galling chain,
  And loud her tocsin blew;
When hoary age became a boy,
And every heart leaped up for joy.

Hail! hail thou glorious day,
  We greet thy blest return,
With speech and gladsome lay,
  And fervent hearts, that burn
To join with those amid the sea,
Whose songs and shouts are Liberty!

Speed, Lord, the glorious day,
  When o'er our native land
Fond Liberty shall sway
  Her sceptre of command;
And every yoke and galling chain,
Shall vanish 'neath her peaceful reign.

Tribute to Rev. William Paul Quinn.

Late Senior Bishop, African M. E. Church.

eath is the common lot of all,
    Yet nothing do we so much dread;
Nothing, that doth our frames befall,
    From which we shrink as from the
        dead.

Though all familiar with the fact
    That death is everywhere unseen,
Yet from his touch we stagger back,
    And strive to thrust long years between.

But why this weakness on our part?
    And why does nature thus recoil?
And why are we so loath to part
    From this vain world of pain and toil?

This always was a house of death,
    And e'er has been a vale of tears;
Here sorrow mingles with our breath,
    And poisons life in all its years.

And yet from death frail nature shrinks,
    And still the finite man complains,
And e'en the spirit man, that thinks,
    Clings to his prison and his chains.

And why? The vast beyond is dark
    And veiled in deepest mystery,
And reason's lamp reveals no mark
    Decisive of our destiny.

There is but one remedial course,
  By which we may and can obtain
From dread of death a full divorce,
  And evermore absolved remain.

Implicit confidence imposed
  In Jesus, God's anointed Son,
Will fill the heart to doubt disposed
  With deathless joys on earth begun,

For faith in Christ dispels the gloom,
  And hope extends her spotless sails,
And finds with God beyond the doom
  A heaven and life, that never fails.

This mortal shall immortal wear,
  Corruption incorruption take,
And saints of God with Christ shall share
  The boundlessness of his estate.

But why is this fair temple clad
  In these habiliments of woe?
And why are all our faces sad,
  Bereft of their accustomed glow?

And why those dirge tones from the choir,
  And why are all these people here?
What strange and burdensome desire
  Has thus induced them to appear?
Where all doth seemingly partake
  Of some unusual widespread gloom,
That to our awe-struck natures wake
  The sad reflections of the tomb?

With all the dread solemnities
　　Associated with that word,
The severance of affinities,
　　Life-loves and friendships long preferred.

This spreading pall, these gloomy scenes,
　　Those dirge tones falling on the ear,
Are but the more impressive means
　　Of telling us that death is here.

Although no shrouded corpse is brought
　　Within this sacred fane today,
To demonstrate what death hath wrought
　　Upon man's frail impassioned clay;

Yet, to our Zion, death has come,
　　And ta'en away from our embrace
One loved abroad and loved at home,
　　The Father Bishop of our race.

And hence, dear friends, we've come to pay
　　A parting tribute of respect,
And thus our humble offering lay
　　Upon the shrine of God's elect.

Fain would we speak in terms of praise
　　Of one, whose life has been bestowed
In countless efforts to upraise
　　A people, writhing 'neath a load.

As Moses saw, in Egypt's land,
　　The hardships that his people bore,
And rather chose with them to stand
　　Than heir the wealth of Pharaoh's store;

So felt the valiant, youthful Quinn
    When he beheld oppression's horde
(Steeped to the very lips in sin)
    Defile the altars of the Lord.

For Slavery's Pharisaic hand
    Had closed the book of life and light,
And all the churches of our land
    Had bowed submissive to his might.

And there was neither court nor fane
    Where God's lorn sons of ebon hue,
Though ne'er so humble, could obtain
    A place of worship as their due.

And Macedonia's cry was heard
    On every breeze, and everywhere,
"Oh, come and break to us the word
    Of life, and lead our hearts in prayer."

He rose, like the intrepid Paul,
    And in the vigor of his youth,
Resolved, whatever might befall,
    To bear to these the words of truth.

Although his purse was ill-supplied
    With means sufficient for the call,
Yet, he on heavenly grace relied,
    And God, the Lord, arranged it all.

God was his friend, his guard and guide,
    His refuge and his mighty tower,
And well he knew He would provide
    For every need and trying hour;

And hence he left all else behind,
   Save God and His abounding grace,
And started forth to heal and bind
   The bruises of his injured race.

Now, from the dread abyss of time,
   Call back the flight of three-score years
And, lo! all clothed in grace sublime,
   A weird and beardless youth appears.

He's tall, and for commanding mien,
A finer mold is seldom seen;
His brow is high, his locks are jet,
His eyes are fierce, his lips are met.

His words are rapid in their flow,
Confined to neither high nor low,
But of that modulated form
Which always tempers to the storm.

Where'er he moves he rears on high
The ensign of his ministry,
And thousands throng to hear his speech,
And learn whereof he came to teach;
The matchless story of the cross,
Compared to which all else is dross,
Comprise the burden and refrain,
And many hear and hear again.

And wonder at his matchless zeal,
His fervent prayer, his strong appeal,
And as he pictures forth the doom
Of sin, which kills beyond the tomb.

Many are pricked e'en to the heart
And, jailor-like, the cry doth start:
"Sir, to be saved, what shall I do?
For all these burning words are true.

And I am wretched and undone.
O, whither shall I fly to shun
The wrath of an avenging God,
Just retribution's chastening rod?"

He points them to the crimson tide,
And to a Savior crucified,
And says to all: "Repent, believe,
Forsake your sins and you shall live."

And as he goes forth, here and there,
New altars rise up unto prayer;
Though rude and meagre, yet are they
In all things equal to the day.

And as the years move on apace
He stands the center of a race
Whose faces are upturned to God,
Praying heaven to break the rod,
And overturn the powers of sin
And let the jubilant year come in.

Near three-score years on Zion's walls
   A faithful sentinel he stood,
And all his sermons, prayers and calls
   Were mingled with atoning blood.

He was, in truth, a burning light,
And sinners trembled in his sight;
For nothing earthly could deter,
Nor friends persuade him to defer
What duty urged him to perform
In weal or woe, in calm or storm.

But oh! how changed; his raven hair
  Is thin and bleached as white as snow,
His face is furrowed deep with care,
  His frame is weak, his steps are slow.

Thus bowed beneath the weight of years,
  He brings his cross and lays it down
At Jesus' feet 'midst angels' cheers,
  And on his brow receives a crown—

A crown of life, bestud with stars,
  The trophies of his conquest here
Midst earth's interminable wars,
  Where all the foes to life appear.

He conquered in the Christian fight,
  He ran the Christian race and won,
And in the realms of endless light
  Has heard the gladsome sound: "Well done.

Well done, for faithful hast thou been
  O'er all things given to thy care;
Heir of my Father's house, come in,
  And all its blest provisions share."

Although our aged bishop's gone,
  And we on earth shall meet no more,
Yet heaven hath many a vale and lawn,
  And friendships that have gone before—

Gone to the realms of holy love,
  Where all are known and all is fair.
For in our Father's house above
  There are no spirit strangers there.

Though gone from earth he is not dead—
  The great and good they never die;
But when their mortal forms they shed,
  In fadeless youth they bloom on high.

O, could we pass beyond the doom,
  And range through fields, forever fair,
Arrayed in heaven's eternal bloom,
  We'd find our sainted bishop there.

Then, O, my friends, rejoice to know,
Where he has gone we all may go,
And move through heaven as he doth now
With life's fair crown upon our brow.

For heaven's blest plans are ample quite
For all whom mercy doth invite;
And every son of Adam's race
The invitation may embrace.

For in our Father's house there's room
For all his children, all may come.
And crowns there are for all to wear,
And palms there are for all to bear,
And robes there are of radiant hue;
Go up and claim them as your due.

Farewell, dear bishop, till the day
When death shall roll the stone away,
And this poor soul released shall fly
To hail thee in the realms on high.

The Union and the Right.

(A Campaign Song.)

We've placed upon our banner,
  The banner of the free,
Harrison and Morton,
  Success and victory.
And they shall bear our standard
  Throughout the coming fight,
And this shall be our watchword,
  The Union and the Right,
  The Union and the Right,
Harrison and Morton,
  The Union and the Right,

Brave sons of honored sires,
  Well known in days of old,
And tried as in a furnace,
  And found as pure as gold;
Tried 'mid the din of battle,
  Or in the halls of state,
By whatsoever standard,
  The twain were truly great.
And they shall bear our standard
  Throughout the coming fight,
    The Union, etc.

Our coats we've doffed for battle,
  And don't propose to yield
Until the latest foeman
  Is banished from the field.

With Harrison and Morton
    To lead our countless host,
To rally is to conquer,
    With each man at his post.
And they shall bear our standard
    Throughout the coming fight,
    The Union, etc.

Go, bear the news to Grover,
    And tell him that the boys
Are shouting loud for Harrison,
    Are making lots of noise;
And will in next November,
    Unless they're much deceived,
Permit his arduous labors
    To be somewhat relieved,
For Harrison and Morton
    Are leaders in the fight.
And this shall be our watchword,
    The Union, etc.

And tell him that his vetoes
    Don't suit the boys in blue;
As at the time of voting
    He'll find it doubly true;
For he who snubs a soldier
    Shall feel a soldier's wrath,
With many thorns and briars
    Strewn thickly in his path;
For Harrison and Morton, etc.

Take hence that foul bandanna,
    With all its filth and slime,
And give us the starry stripes,
    Flag of our olden time;

Then with our gallant leader,
  The son of Tippecanoe,
We'll show you in November
  What patriots can do.
For Harrison and Morton
  Are leaders in this fight,
And this shall be our watchword:
  The Union and the Right.

Song for the First Day of August.

With cheerful hearts we've come
  From many a happy home,
    Our friends to greet;
  And pass a social hour
  Beneath this leafy bower,
Where many a shrub and flower
    In fragrance meet.

We come to joy with those
Whose gloomy night of woes
Have past away,
And render worthy meeds
To men whose noble deeds
First cast the genial seeds
  Of Liberty.

Then let our heart's best song
In acclamations strong,
  Reach heaven's height,
In honor of that hour
When Slavery's massive tower
Crumble beneath the power
  Of truth and right.

This is proud Freedom's day!
Swell, swell the gladsome lay,
  Till earth and sea
Shall echo with the strain,
Through Britain's vast domain;
No bondman clanks his chain,
  All men are free.

God hasten on the time
When Slavery's blighting crime
  And curse shall end;
When man may widely roam
Beneath the arching dome,
And find with man a home,
  In man a friend.

Descriptive Voyage from New York to Aspinwall.

Farewell, for now my gallant bark,
    Loosed from her mooring, quits the
      shore
Amid a fog and mist as dark
    As that which spread old Egypt o'er.

On this black and fearful night,
    She dare not venture out to sea
Lest on some rock or reef she might,
    At early dawn, all foundered be.

The white cap's surges bear aloft
    Our vessel, in the murky air,
Then down within the sea's deep trough
    She's plunged, but not to linger there,

But she was built to brave the wind
And mountain billows all combined,
And while she feels their angry tread,
They bring to her no gloomy dread.

Hence till the mist and fog had fled;
Until the morning rays had spread
Her genial rays o'er land and tide,
My anchored bark doth proudly ride.

'Tis morn and now my goodly ship,
 With spreading canvas all unfurled,
Like frighted deer doth bound and skip;
 Old Neptune's waves doth proudly hurl,

While smiles of peace and calm resign
 Paints every cheek or decks the brow;
And of the Hundreds none repine,
 But all seems resignation now.

A steady, brisk, increasing gale
Spreads to the compass all our sail
And bears us o'er the trackless main
From friends we hope to meet again.

'Tis night and now, if forged in wrath
 And on destruction's errand sent,
The mountain waves that sweep our path
 Could scarcely be more violent;

But while she reels thus to and fro
 The sickest of the sick am I
And from my system would I throw
 It's last contents, or even die.

Oh, of all that's known or heard
 Of sickness in its varied form,
The last of all to be preferred
 Is sea sick-sickness in a storm.

Too sick to live, nor can we tell
Why in this neither state we dwell,
For life seems scarcely worth the breath
That severs our sad state from death.

And were it not for superstition,
   We'd claim some Jonah somewhere stored;
And yet 'tis true our sad condition
   Changed not till one leaped over board.

Yes, on that night of winds and tide,
   One poor unfortunate and unknown
Leaped from our vessel's wave-washed side
   And found his coral bed alone.

O! Thou eternal mystery,
Thou grand, sublime, though awful sea,
Alas, how oft thy fury smothers
The last fond hope of wives and mothers.

'Tis morn the fourth and calm's the sea
   As though some talesmanic wand
Had quelled the waves inebriety
   By virtue of the wielder's hand;

For e'er had bloomed the misty morn,
   Fair Luna sweeping o'er the main
Had caught the fierce winds in her horn,
   And bound the mad waves with a chain.

Then old Atlantic calmed his raid,
As though some shrewd Philistine maid
Had won his heart and ta'en away
His bristling waves and angry spray—

'Tis moonlight on the deep blue sea,
   And, skimming o'er the curling wave,
My gallant bark moves blithe and free
   As mind could wish or heart could crave.

Nor lays she for the sluggish breeze
   That fain would seek a night's repose.
Impelled by steam she beats the seas,
   With her huge arm thus on she goes.

And bears me toward that sunny clime,
Where grows the orange and the lime
And flowers of every varied hue
From lily white to violet blue.

'Tis morn the seventh and the last,
   And here my Baltic voyage must end;
Through calms and storms and death she's past
   To reach this hot and sultry clime;

For Aspinwall is a sultry place,
   Where noxious vapors taint the air,
And peopled by a tribal race
   Most thinly clad with little care;

And yet the denizens you find
Residing here are wondrous kind,
And versed in many a tender word
By which the heart to love is stirred.

Yet Aspinwall's a sultry place,
   For here the sunshine and the rain
Meet each other and embrace
   As lovers do,—then part again.

For, in the space of one brief hour,
The sun will shine and then a shower
Of rain will fall so thick and fast,
You'd think the clouds would weep their last.

But O, if in her gorgeous dress,
Nature in all her loveliness
The world encomium should command,
'Tis on this narrow frith of land;

For rarer fruits and fairer flowers
Scarce ever bloomed in Eden bowers,
Than bud and bloom and ripen here
Through all the seasons of the year.

For there's no rose without a thorn,
    Nor much of joy without regret;
For where our brightest hopes are born,
    Sad disappointments oft are met.

Nor have we an exception found
    In this bright land, so seeming fair,
For here, while beauty paints the ground,
    A foul miasma taints the air;
And dread malaria's poisoned breath,
Spread far and wide the fumes of death,

And oft so direful in their sway,
That hundreds perish in a day.
O Land of sunshine and of showers,
Of rarest fruits and fairest flowers,

Adieu! Adieu, for at the quay
A vessel waits to bear away,
Not only me, but many a score
That fain would leave thy fevered shore.

Paddle Your Own Canoe.

 Red chief dwelling near a lake,
  Beneath a Western sky,
Felt soon his hold on life must break,
  And he lay down and die—

He called around his wigwam door
  His warriors, brave and true,
And gave to each a tiny oar,
  Saying: "Paddle your own canoe,"

For I, your Brave, who taught the bow
  And how to poise the dart,
And how the bearded shaft to throw
  With many a needful art,

Am full of years and cannot stand
  As I were wont to do;
I soon must try the spirit land,
  So, "Paddle your own canoe."

Then lowly bowed each warrior's head,
  And a deep long sigh he drew;
They started forth with measured tread,
  To paddle their own canoe.

High rose the waves on either side,
  Loud screamed the wild sea mew;
But naught could daunt their warrior pride,
  They paddled their own canoe.

O'er rugged heights they onward sped,
  And mazy forests through,
And whereso'er their duty led,
  They paddled their own canoe.

And oft in fancy's bark they'd speed
  Back through the waters blue,
And once again their chieftain heed
  Saying: "Paddle your own canoe."

Should friends forsake, should fortune fail
  Or loved ones prove untrue,
Then nerve your heart and courage take,
  And paddle your own canoe.

For the world with many a snare is set
  For the honest and the true,
And they alone escape the net,
  Who paddle their own canoe.

Valedictory on Leaving San Francisco, California.

here is no cord, however strong,
    That time will not its fibers rend,
Nor weary road, however long,
    But constant march will find its end.

As with the cord, and with the road,
    E'en so with all our friendships here,
Howe'er so worthily bestowed;
    Our loves may be as fond and dear;

We deem the object of our trust;
    There is a time, and come it must,
An hour of parting on the wing,
    And friendship's heart must feel the sting.

For life is one continuous change;
    There's nothing stable, nothing sure,
Nothing in all our mortal range
    That we can grasp and feel secure.

The rose will wither in its prime,
    The violet droop its head and die,
The century oak, at touch of time
    Will prostrate, fall and mouldering lie.

And e'en the granite by the shore,
Lashed by the mad waves evermore,
Will waste away, grain after grain,
Till nothing of the rock remain.

And yet, with all these facts at hand,
　　How friends, solicitous are we,
Weaving with care the silken band
　　As though 'twas for eternity.

What pains we take to mold a friend,
　　To stamp our image on the heart;
And e'er the anxious task we end,
　　Stern fate, or duty, bids us part.

Alas! how weather-like is life;
　　Eternal sunshine is unknown.
Our joys and sorrows room with strife,
　　And we alternate, laugh and mourn.

Alas! alas! how much we owe
To that of which we little know.
The circumstances of an hour,
These, these are far beyond our power.

And yet in these we widely roam,
　　Or owe to them our lengthened stay;
And few within this sacred dome,
　　Who have not yielded to their sway.

E'en 'gainst the teachings of their youth;
　　Against the pledges of the soul;
Against the urgencies of truth,
　　How oft we've bowed to their control.

Nor will time affect their claim,
But all through life will wield the same
Matchless power and mystic spell,
Producing many a sad farewell.

Farewell, oh land of my sojourn!
And you, the many friends I've met;
My wandering footsteps homeward turn,
With joys commingled with regret.

I joy in sweet, prospective bliss,
Of meeting soon the loved and true,
And sigh for friendships I shall miss
In bidding this fair land adieu.

But ocean waves, nor time nor place,
Can e'er from memory's page erase
The kindly acts and friendly care,
Bestowed, since first I landed here.

I came a stranger to your land,
A wanderer from a foreign shore,
With neither card nor scrip in hand
Your recognition to secure;

But he who cares for finite dust,
The wise, the infinite, the just,
Has willed each humble heart a friend
Where'er his wandering footsteps tend.

And I have met upon your shore
The willing hand and open door,
And many a word of kindly cheer
Has greeted my arrival here.

Farewell! farewell! the hour has come!
The ship that waits to bear me home
Lies anchored in her berth at bay;
And soon, as dashing through the foam,
And peradventure through the storm,
She'll bear me on my homebound way.

Yet, on and on till the land shall die,
And nothing save the sea and sky
Shall come within my vision's range;
Not e'en a bird to mar or change
E'en for a moment's space of time
The all monotonous, sublime!

Yet on, and on, with my trust in Him
Who laid His hand on the ocean's brim,
And said to the rolling waves: "Be still!"
And the wind and waves obeyed His will;
Then trustingly on o'er the restless tide,
On to the land of my youthful pride!
Then joyously on o'er the glorious earth,
Till my feet shall stand on my homestead
        hearth.

But should occasion e'er recall
    The memory of my presence here;
If from your annual festive hall
    Is missed the shattered voice you hear;
Know that that voice, if vocal, still
Its humble mission to fulfil,
Somewhere, in God's great providence,
Is trilling in the poor's defense.

Farewell, farewell! my task is o'er;
    And if on earth I meet you never,
Then, then upon that pearly shore,
    Where time cannot our friendships sever,
Where fadeless blooms the tree of life,
Where enters never care nor strife,
There may I meet you, every one,
Father, mother, daughter, son,
Where never shall rise from the notes that swell,
The heartrending sighs of a sad farewell.

Banishment of Man from the Garden of the Lord.

Dedicated to Rev. William S. Bradden as a tribute to one who has served his God, his Country and his fellow Man with unceasing Devotion, Patriotism and Love.

oll back, O Muse! and with the dawn
　　Of Time's young morn's benignant
　　　　lay,
　　Begin when first, o'er Eden's lawn
　　Our unborn parents led their way.

Sing of their peaceful, blest abode;
　　Sing of the joy-pervading stream,
Which through their sinless bosoms flowed,
　　And swept life onward like a dream.

While from each fragrant shrub and flower
　　The perfumed zephyrs, in their flight,
Bore on their wings, from bower to bower,
　　Undying odors of delight.

And there, midst trees of mighty root,
　　Forever robed in fadeless green,
And groaning 'neath ambrosial fruit,
　　Bright heavenly visitants were seen.

These perchance had been their guest,
　　Their comrades, when all else alone,
Since every land alike was blest
　　Where e'er the bright Shekina shone.

These may have passed their noonday hours,
In strolling o'er the fleecy sward
Amidst those bright unfolding flowers,
The care of Eden's youthful lord.

Pure Seraphims and Angels bright
In social intercourse with man;
What glorious ages of delight,
How worthy of a lengthened span.

Behold their beauty unadorned;
Think of their love without alloy;
Conceive a brow that ne'er had scorned,
Then mingle peace with boundless joy.

And lo, we've nothing save a shadow,
And dim as to the palefaced moon,
Gazing on the surging billow
Becomes the joys of yester noon.

Behold the vast provisions made
In vastness vast, yet how complete;
Of every tree, 'midst bower and glade,
Save one, they might at pleasure eat.

But, in the midst and towering high,
The tree of Evil and of Good
Proved more seductive to the eye
Than all the trees of Eden's wood.

This was the Interdicted Tree,
Of which 'twas said: "Thou shall not eat,"
And if thou dost, the penalty
Shall be thy Death! a judgment meet.

Thus stood that tree a living proof
   As loyalty to heaven's throne,
And while man kept from thence aloof
   God's smiling brow approval shone.

But when, regardless of his fate,
   Regardless of the fell decree,
Man took therefrom the fruit and ate,
   The brow of Heaven grew wrathfully.

Alas! alas! the deed was done;
Their peace was slain, their grief begun:
They scarce knew why, yet in their breast
They felt a strange and sad unrest.

Oppressed with grief, distressed with fear,
They bend to earth their weary ear
To catch that step when far away,
That came with each declining day.

At length they raise their grief-bowed head
   In hope that angel friends were nigh;
But lo, the sinless host had fled
   Back to their mansion in the sky,

To show that Heaven no commerce hath,
   With felons doomed, within the pit
Those erring miscreants of wrath
   On whom the seal of Death is set.

The die was cast; 'gainst God's command,
   Forever firm and ever just,
Earth's crowned Lord had raised His hand
   And doomed the breathing world to dust.

They stand awhile in deep amaze,
Then from the sun's refulgent blaze,
And from their God's omniscient eye,
Amid the tangled wood they fly,

And vainly hope some screen to find
Where guilt and shame might lurk behind,
And where the twain themselves might hide;
But conscience stands on every side
And scans them with his eyes of flame
That spoke their guilt, and breathed their shame.

An Angel seeks them midst the wood
    And drags them to their judgment room;
The trembling, dark, expectant mood
    In which they come bespeak their doom.

In open court the Judge now reads
    The charge and cause of their arrest,
To all of which he *Guilty!* pleads
    And yields him back his Crown and Crest.

Then Justice grasped his gleaming sword,
    All keenly drawn from point to hilt,
And waits the bidding of his Lord
    To expiate the culprit's guilt.

But Mercy now doth intervene
And steps within the breach between
The offended Judge and culprits twain,
And bares his bosom to be slain.

A deathlike silence now ensues,
While every eye amazement glues
Upon that mediatorial face,
Embodiment of every grace.

Mercy at length the silence breaks,
And for the Crownless Monarch makes
A plea that melts the Court to tears,
And moves the heart of all that hears,

But Justice with relentless ire
Doth still for sin a life require,
Whereon the Judge upon the throne
Hold pleading Mercy to atone,

And then commutes the dire intent
To that of toil and banishment.
They hear their doom without a sigh
Or e'en a tear to dim the eye:

For they had reached that stage of grief
Where tears could bring them no relief.
The Arrest—The Charge—The Penalty
Had followed each so rapidly
That there had been no time for thought
Upon their strange and arduous lot.

Perhaps their feet had never trod
Beyond the pleasant walks of God:
Their morn, their noon, their evening hours
Had all been spent mid Eden's bowers.

Sweet peace had dwelt their bowers among
And holy love their praise had sung;
They ne'er had heard the angry wail
Of nature warring with the gale,
Nor lions roar, the panther's yell,
Had on their listening organs fell.

The Shades of night were hovering nigh,
    All ready with their sable pall
To robe the earth and veil the sky,
    And shroud in darkness one and all.

And yet they stand in dread suspense,
Till Pity kindly leads them hence,
And fitting robes for each prepare
To brave a less salubrious air.

'Tis done! and yielding to their fate,
They move in silence toward the gate:
The Angel follows in command,
To watch and guard with sword in hand.

The exit gained, they're driven hence
Amid a darkness most intense;
No hand to guide, no angel voice
To urge them to the better choice;

But hand in hand, together they
Groped through the night their dubious way—
Huge spectral forms before them rise
Like hideous monsters to the skies,

While prowling beasts in quest of prey
Fill night with terror and dismay;
O! how dreadful must have been,
That first night, in a world of sin.

Fain would they to their lost estate
Return; but lo, within the gate,
Bearing commission from his Lord,
An angel waves a flaming sword.

They linger long anear the gate,
Feeding the hope that soon, or late,
Some angel friend will intercede
And in their cause so ably plead—
As to revoke the dread decree
That binds them to their destiny.

But when at length their hopes grew faint
They turned away without complaint
And soon were wrapped in sleep profound
Upon the bare, untented ground.

But while they lay unconscious there,
A vision bright and passing fair
Bends over them, and kindly words of cheer
Breathes softly in their slumbering ear:
"Be not afraid, for lo, 'tis I,
To whom thy every groan and sigh
Are Known. Go forth with cheer,
And lo, I am forever near."

The vision past, at morn they rise,
And hail the day with glad surprise,
To find the burden of their woes
All vanished, with the night's repose.

While ever and anon they hear
Reverberating in their ear—
Go forth with cheer!
For lo, I am forever near.

Their few effects, their meagre store
Is soon arranged; this being o'er
Toward Eden's bowers, now still in view,
They turn and bid a last adieu.

With hope alert, with fears subdued,
They brave the pathless solitude,
While ever and anon they hear
Reverberating in their ear—
Lo, I am forever near.

And as the years rolled on apace
They stand the center of a race,
Expansive as the rays of light,
And numerous as the stars of night.

The wilderness has been subdued,
And through the pathless solitude
A highway has been built, the rocks between
The which no vulture's eye has seen
Nor lion's whelp had ever trod,
Built for the ransomed of the Lord.

And on and down the flight of years
They pass, and lo a Star appears,
To nightly watchers on the plains
Heralded by sweet Angelic Strains,

And from the radiance of the Sheen
Come forth the form of matchless mein
And to the awe struck watchers said
Be not afraid, for lo, I bring
Glad tidings of your promised King.

For unto you on this blest morn,
In David's house, a child is born,
The promised Seed, the blest reward,
A Saviour, which is Christ the Lord.

Go forth, and Heaven shall lend a ray
To guide you on your joyous way,
And in a manger you shall find
The Infant Saviour of mankind;

For He His people shall redeem,
And He shall reign a King, supreme;
Before Him every knee shall bend,
And Countless years His reign extend.

And as the angel host went back,
To Heaven, along the shining track,
They tuned their harps, they struck their lyre,
And sang as sang the heavenly choir.

For every Harp in Heaven was strung,
And every voice loud anthems sung,
In honor of the wondrous birth
Of Christ, The King and Prince of Heaven and
        Earth.

Acrostic.

Moments of youth, oh, how swiftly they roll,
And yet they are priceless as mountains of gold.
Redeem them, redeem them, oh don't let them fly,
You never can recall them,when once they pass by.
Jewels, though rare, may be lost in the sand;
And others obtained from a far distant land.
Not so with youth's moments; when once they are
     gone,
Even thus they'll remain, till eternity's dawn.
Wisdom, bless'd wisdom, she speaks unto all,
In the summer of life, prepare for the fall.
Like apples of silver, or pictures of gold,
So prize the rich moments of youth as they roll.
Oh! lady remember, the diamond that shines,
No beauty reveals until dug from the mines.

Sonnet.

God is and is seen wherever we look,
    From the roaring sea to the noiseless
      brook;
    From the everlasting snow-clad hill,
    To the smallest sand beneath the rill.
The granite rock and the liquid flood,
Each portray the living hand of God!
From the blazing sun that rules the day,
To the faint light of the glow worm's ray;
From the blue vaults of the azure sky,
From all the nocturnal worlds on high;
To the smallest insects on the ground,
Wherever that insect may be found,
The daguerreotype of God is there,
Insects, stars and sky and sun declare.

Acrostic.

Sweet lady, I would sing to thee,
Of genial spring and summer's bloom,
Plenteous autumn, rich and free,
Hoary winter with all its gloom.
In this thy spring, thy morn of life,
At once for coming time prepare,
For summer days are fraught with strife,
Ripe autumn brings on whitened hair;
And oh! may fall and winter be
No less joyous than thy spring.
Contentment, peace and pleasure see,
In serving God, and sweetly sing.
Substantial joys doth Jesus bring.

A Bridal Toast.

ay thy hopes never be blasted;
   May thy joys never cease;
   May thy love be true and lasting,
   And day by day increase.

May prudence forever guard thee,
   Contentment be thy friend;
May health strew roses 'round thee,
   And thy peace never end.

As the lark that hails the morning
   With songs so blythe and gay,
As the doves that woo the evening,
   May thy hours pass away.

When the lark shall seek the willow,
   And the dove ceases her cries,
Go thou, then to thy downy pillow,
   Go! dream of Paradise.

INDEX.